Succeed at Negotiating

Succeed at Negotiating

Effective techniques to secure the results you want

KEN LANGDON

LONDON, NEW YORK,
MUNICH, MELBOURNE, DELHI

Project Editor	Tom Broder
Project Art Editor	Edward Kinsey
Editor	Elizabeth Watson
Senior Editor	Simon Tuite
Senior Art Editor	Sara Robin
Assistant Designer	Kathryn Wilding
DTP Designer	Traci Salter
Production Controller	Stuart Masheter
Picture Researcher	Sarah Hopper
Special Photography	Roger Dixon
Executive Managing Editor	Adèle Hayward
Managing Art Editor	Karla Jennings
Art Director	Peter Luff
Publisher	Corinne Roberts

First American Edition, 2007
Published in the United States by
DK Publishing, 375 Hudson Street,
New York, NY 10014

07 08 09 10 10 9 8 7 6 5 4 3 2 1

A Cataloging-in-Publication record for this book is available from the Library of Congress.

ISBN 978-0-75662-613-6

ED247
Printed and bound in China by Leo Paper Group

Contents

3 **Set Up Meetings**

4 **Manage Your Negotiation**

5 **Manage the Conclusion**

Introduction

No organization can succeed without effective negotiators. Indeed, no human interaction can thrive without compromise and an ability to recognize win/win situations. Understanding negotiation is, therefore, a key competency not only for people who need to negotiate with customers, suppliers, and the other side in industrial relations, but for anyone whose job includes seeking agreement with other people.

Professional negotiators understand the importance of thorough preparation. They know how to set their objectives and plan the form and timing of concessions, and how to make the granting of concessions conditional on getting what they want in return. They also understand the process of negotiation, from the initial planning stages and the period spent looking for advantage, through to the process of conceding reluctantly and closing effectively. So, whether you are negotiating with your boss for a raise, closing an important account, or working out the

final terms and conditions for supplying products to a customer, you need to develop your negotiating skills to make sure that you get the best deal available.

Succeed at Negotiating helps you to assess your current negotiating skills and then looks at every aspect of negotiation, achieving your objectives, and considering the long term. It takes you from preparing your arguments and setting up negotiating meetings to managing your way through a professional negotiating process to achieve an excellent result. It also shows you maneuvers and tactics that improve your position, weaken your opponent's, and help you time your closing bid. Specially commissioned photographs illustrate the subtle visual signals that people send and show you how to interpret and select the right technique for the right moment. There are also invaluable case studies, techniques that you can practice in your everyday life, professional tips, and special features on key aspects of the negotiating process—in short, everything you need to become a top negotiator.

Negotiation is the art of finding a favorable compromise

Assessing Your Skills

The aim of this questionnaire is to get you to think about your negotiating skills and assess your scope for improvement, so answer honestly. Complete it before reading the book, choosing the answer that comes closest to your preferred response, and putting the appropriate letter in the "Before" box. After you have read the book and applied the techniques, complete the questionnaire a second time.

Before After

1 What attitude do you take in negotiations?

A You want a fast result, so you make it obvious that you will compromise.
B You look and sound as tough as possible so that they can see you will not give way.
C You aim for a mutually acceptable conclusion.

2 Do you understand the principle of exchange?

A You are not sure what it is.
B You know that everything comes at a price.
C It is when one party will make a concession in exchange for the other party's doing the same.

3 How flexible do you expect the people who you negotiate with to be?

A They never give anything away.
B You expect a bit of give and take.
C If they've agreed to negotiate, they have room for maneuver; your job is to identify and obtain all the available concessions.

4 How clearly do you set your objectives?

A Your objective is to get the best possible deal.
B You know one or two main must-haves.
C You list your objectives and have targets.

Before After

5 Who do you involve in the negotiation?

A There's only one important person—the person with the authority to make concessions.
B You keep your own people informed.
C You try to talk to all stakeholders on both sides.

6 How important is it to obtain your best possible outcome?

A You are not sure what that means.
B If you do not get your best possible outcome, you feel that you have lost the negotiation.
C You take the attitude that anything you get above the least you would settle for is a bonus.

7 How much intelligence do you obtain on the other side's objectives and limits?

A They're not going to tell you their limits, so you doubt you'll be able to find out much.
B You probe for these during your meetings.
C You make a list of what you believe will be their demands and adjust them as you learn more.

8 How often do you demand a concession in return for one of yours?

A You don't; if you give in, you've lost that point.
B Whenever you can.
C You only give a concession if you get one back.

9 Do you try to involve senior managers?

A No, it's your job to get the best deal.
B If you have to, you ask them to take over.
C You involve senior managers to emphasize the importance you attach to a deal.

10 Do you use role-play to rehearse situations?

A You don't rehearse at all.
B You mentally work through possible situations.
C You use structured role-play to work through possible scenarios with fellow team members.

		Before	After
11	**Do you plan your concessions in advance?** **A** No—you won't know what they want until you have started negotiating. **B** You know your limits in the main areas. **C** You plan concessions thoroughly, and try to plan when to introduce each concession.		
12	**In how much detail do you prepare your negotiating objectives and strategy?** **A** You prefer to react to options as they come up. **B** You have a firm aiming point, but don't really plan the steps to get there. **C** You think through a step-by-step strategy, but keep it short and flexible to handle surprises.		
13	**Do you try to propose the agenda?** **A** You dislike agendas—they are too prescriptive. **B** You don't think it matters who proposes it as long as it covers all the points. **C** You always propose the agenda so that you can control when each item will be discussed.		
14	**Do you make the first proposal or respond to their proposal?** **A** You always try to get your proposal in first. **B** You prefer to respond rather than propose; this way you learn where they're coming from. **C** It depends on circumstances.		

Final Scores

	A	B	C
Before			
After			

Analysis

Mostly As

Your answers suggest that you are fairly new to negotiating and, while you may be enthusiastic, you need to think about the basic techniques of professional negotiating and the negotiation process. Think first about your preparation and plan more before you start the negotiation. Then work on the process to make sure you understand each stage. Think more carefully about your opponents and what their objectives are, and carefully consider your own.

Mostly Bs

You have some knowledge of professional negotiating and deal with your opponents quite well. You are starting to see the negotiation from the other party's point of view, but you need to put more time and energy into improving your skills in this area. Start with one opponent and one negotiation and plan your way through each stage of the negotiation process. Be self-critical of your overall approach to setting a strategy, to ensure that you get to the best possible position.

Mostly Cs

You certainly have a professional approach to your role as negotiator. Make sure, however, that you also establish good rapport with your opponents. Concentrate on your long-term strategy with people you negotiate with frequently, and use some of the techniques in this book to build mutually-acceptable results. Use these techniques to assist other people in your team to improve their skills. Show them how important it is to have open and honest contact with their opponents.

Conclusion

If this is the first time you have done this self-assessment, then bear in mind the above analysis as you read the book. Pay special attention to the areas highlighted by your responses and take on board the tips and techniques—these will help you to achieve a more balanced mixture of B and C answers next time around. After you have read the book and had a chance to put the techniques into practice, take the quiz again. Provided you have answered honestly, you will able to measure your progress. You should see a big improvement!

1 Get Yourself Ready

We all spend a lot of time and effort negotiating, whether with friends and family, with colleagues, or with customers. Negotiating is the art of reaching a compromise that suits both parties. It is also a contest where people try to achieve the best result for themselves. To help you appreciate and develop the right attitude to succeed, this chapter shows you how to:

- Understand what negotiation involves and which key skills are important for success
- Recognize the different possible outcomes from negotiation and know what to aim for
- Learn how effective preparation can help you negotiate from a position of strength.

Define Negotiation

Negotiation occurs when someone can supply an item or service that you want and that you are prepared to bargain for in order to achieve an acceptable resolution.

Understand the Need for Negotiation

Negotiation is a peaceful way to resolve a conflict. In politics, religion, or sports, parties with conflicting ideas may simply agree to differ. However, when a difference of opinion occurs between a child and parent, for example, the respective parties have to negotiate a resolution acceptable to both sides. Statesmen negotiate complex international agreements, trade unions and employers are more or less in continuous negotiations, and partners in long-term relationships know they must negotiate or face difficulties.

Negotiation is the movement of two parties toward each other's position

Seek Agreement

Negotiations are about two sides moving toward each other's position until they reach agreement. As a trade union leader put it, "The employers and I are in a negotiation, walking toward each other; my job is to make them walk a little faster than me." But the aim of negotiation is agreement. Both sides wish to reach a conclusion in a reasonable amount of time and certainly in

Overlap for Negotiation

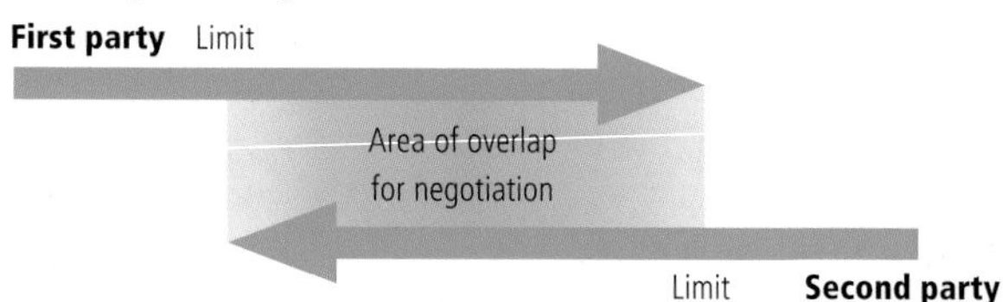

Know the Limits In well-prepared negotiations, each side understands where their absolute limits lie. Negotiation discovers where these limits overlap.

Let us never negotiate out of fear. But let us never fear to negotiate.

John F. Kennedy

time for the agreement to be put into practice. If a salesperson and a future customer do not negotiate to achieve an acceptable compromise, then the salesperson will not take an order and the customer will not get the product. Both sides will waste all the time and resources they have put into the project thus far.

Develop a positive attitude to negotiating by looking for areas where you agree with the other party. If you take a suspicious attitude into the negotiation and emphasize your unwillingness to compromise, you are unlikely to achieve the outcome you seek. If you strive for agreement at every opportunity, you are more likely to come to a quick and effective conclusion.

Informal Negotiations Recognize the informal negotiating situations that occur with friends and family. Identify key skills and techniques you can transfer to more formal situations.

Consider the Other Party

There are at least two sides to every negotiation. Just as you will seek to take a confident and assertive approach when negotiating, so will your opponent. You should try to be as interested in the other party's point of view as your own. If you learn to put yourself in their shoes, you will find it much easier to evaluate the strengths and weaknesses of their position and appreciate where you need to compromise.

Know When to Negotiate

In business you can negotiate for everything. You will frequently hear salespeople and others declare that head-quarters sets the price and they have no ability to alter it. Frequently this is not true. If a customer tells a salesperson that it is company policy to buy from a competitor, then

TECHNIQUES *to* practice

The ability to stay in control during negotiations is an important skill to learn so your body language doesn't undermine your message. People often show their feelings as they discuss or negotiate issues with friends and family—for example, by showing frustration or impatience if they are not getting their own way. In everyday life there are occasions when you can practice staying in control. For example, if your partner or child is taking a long time to get ready, try the following approaches:

1 Stay completely calm—this gives you authority and allows you to think more rationally and argue a more logical case.
2 Adopt a "poker face"—hiding emotions such as frustration prevents revealing a weakness and makes people more likely to cooperate with you.

TIP Always assume that the other party is well prepared for the negotiation.

Effective Ways to Negotiate with Children

HIGH IMPACT

- Praising children for making a concession
- Explaining logic in their terms
- Being consistent and setting consistent boundaries

NEGATIVE IMPACT

- Answering a question with "because I said so"
- Refusing to take time to explain
- Negotiating different limits on different days

---

the salesperson must first suspect that the customer could vary the policy. If this really isn't the case, the salesperson must find the particular person who set the policy, and persuade them to change it. In your personal life, the instances of negotiation may be more informal, but they offer just as many opportunities. The key point to keep in mind is that any negotiation, whatever the circumstances, should always be about reaching an outcome that is acceptable to both parties.

Learn from Children

Children quickly develop considerable negotiating skills. From learning how much noise earns how much food, they quickly move on to negotiate the ratio of vegetables to ice cream they are prepared to eat in their diet. Indeed, in many ways children are much better negotiators than adults: they have fewer inhibitions and are prepared to use any means available to them in order to get what they want. Adults lose some of these negotiating advantages as their perceptions change. Many successful negotiators use an affable and friendly adult style, while underneath they retain a childlike determination to achieve the best result for themselves. Children have a weakness in negotiating, however, that you can learn from: their voice and body language tend to show what they are thinking. In contrast, adult negotiators develop a "poker face" that gives away as few clues as possible, making it harder for their opponents to predict their next move.

Aim for Success

There are three possible outcomes of a negotiation: win/win, win/lose, and lose/lose. The ideal is that both sides are equally satisfied in the long term.

Achieve Win/Win

In most sports, one side wins and the other loses, but negotiation is a different type of contest—the aim is for both sides to believe that they have won a good deal. Win/win does not mean that no sacrifices are made, but that there is equality of pain on both sides: by conceding in one area, they have gained value in another. If a trade unionist wins a pay deal higher than the rate of inflation, the management must feel that they have received an increase in productivity in exchange.

Avoid Win/Lose

One of the worst long-term results of a negotiation is for one side to feel as though the other has taken advantage of them. Such a win/lose outcome remains in the losing person's mind for a long time; it is human nature for the losing party to resolve to get the opposite result the next time such a negotiation takes place. Win/lose is often followed by lose/win and is ultimately in nobody's interests.

think SMART

While a win/win outcome is most desirable, in some cases it may be appropriate to settle for a win/lose result, if this fits in with your broader strategy.

For example, a supplier may sell a product or service below cost if they want to prove their ability to a new customer, undercut the competition, or hold on to a long-term relationship in a buyer's market. Losing the battle in one negotiation may help toward your overall plan. Such an approach depends on where the power lies between parties.

Look for Win/Win

Different organizations have different priorities. This can be useful because it offers opportunities for each organization to trade low-priority concessions for more significant ones.

Always look for issues that are major to one party but minor to the other. Take the example of a small business selling to a large one:

- ➔ Cash flow is a major issue in a small business, but in large organizations managers tend not to have cash-flow targets, so they could offer early payment in exchange for concessions.
- ➔ In small organizations, customer service often requires less in the way of infrastructure, so the small business may be happy to offer free after-sales care in exchange for other concessions.

Relationship Management

You may need to negotiate with the same people in the future, so it is worth investing the time to build social relationships and find win/win outcomes.

Conclude Effectively

The aim of a negotiation is success, where both parties feel that they have concluded a good deal. It is based on the principle of exchange—one party will give something in exchange for the other party's giving something. Timing can play a significant role. You should try to keep the end point of a negotiation as open as possible to avoid being put in the position of having to reach a conclusion at a particular time. People tend to rush to unwise concessions if they are faced with a deadline. This is something you can use to your advantage, but equally, you need to be aware of the possibility that people will use this tactic against you. Indeed, it is not uncommon for people hosting international negotiations to offer to book the return flights of their visitors who coming to their country for talks. The resident team can then use an array of tactics to delay any serious negotiation until the departure hour approaches. This puts the visiting team at a considerable disadvantage.

CASE study: Avoiding lose/lose

Nitin was negotiating for Bill's band to play at his wedding. They had agreed on the price and when the band would play. But there was a problem with accommodations: Bill believed Nitin should pay for the band's hotel rooms, whereas Nitin thought, late though it would be, the band could go home. They asked Celia to join them. Celia summarized the points already agreed and suggested they either compromise or come to the conclusion that they could not find an agreeable deal. Faced with failure, Nitin and Bill quickly agreed to split the cost of the rooms.

- *Both parties felt that the question of accommodations was an important issue, and neither was willing to concede. For either party to have overruled the other person's objections would have meant a win/lose result, which would have bred resentment, or else failure to reach an agreement at all—a lose/lose result.*
- *Celia's intervention helped Nitin and Bill to recognize that mutual concessions were the only realistic alternative to simply walking away from the deal. The summary of their positions helped them to achieve a win/win outcome.*

Recognize When to Walk Away

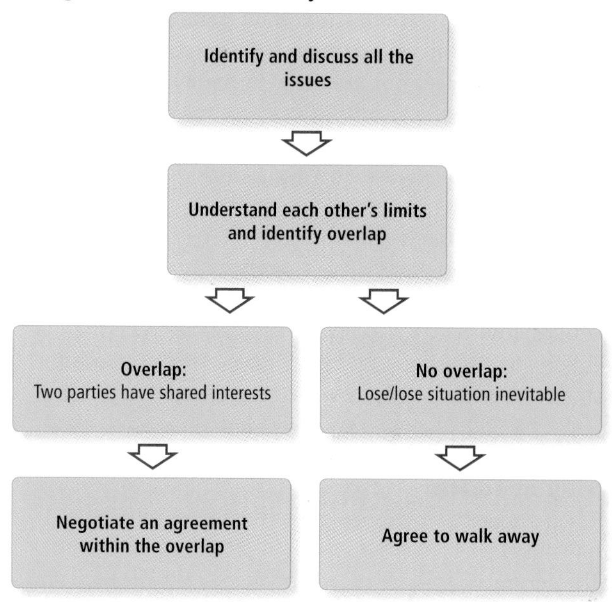

Recognize Lose/Lose

A negotiation that ends without agreement is almost certainly a lose/lose result. It means that an intention to come to a mutually satisfactory conclusion has failed. Yet this may, from time to time, be an appropriate outcome. Suppose that you are trying to make a business case for your company to invest in a new distribution system with automation in your warehouse. It may become obvious during the negotiation that the only way the business case will make sense is if the supplier cuts their price to well below their normal profit margin. It is plainly sensible for both parties to reluctantly walk away from the deal. You were serious in your intention to investigate the project thoroughly, but the lose/lose outcome could be worse for both parties if a deal is struck: the supplier will resent the effort put into installation, and you will face a very marginal, and therefore risky, business case.

Use Agents Effectively

You can use professional negotiating skills by engaging agents to get the best deal possible on your behalf. But remember, price is not as crucial to them as it is to you.

Brief Comprehensively

If you use a professional negotiator, such as a real estate agent to sell your property, it is important to brief them carefully, particularly about price and time scale. The agent needs to present a price low enough to attract potential buyers and to make a sale quickly, but high enough for you to profit financially. Watch out for agents who deliberately overprice your property to get you to use their services; but do look for optimistic agents who will set about finding a buyer in a positive fashion.

Stay in Touch

If you are working with an agent to make a purchase, remember that their purpose in business is to make a deal. They normally operate on a percentage of the transaction price, so a drop in price will have far more impact on you than on an agent who is working for a fee of 6 percent. Stay in touch with your agent, as the situation is fluid until contracts are signed. For example, if another buyer comes into the picture you may have to increase your offer.

think SMART

Look for hidden opportunities when negotiating: a deal is not done until the ink is dry on the contract.

For example, if you are buying a suit and you agree on a price, do not hesitate to reopen the price negotiation if you buy another item. This can be a good strategy in many situations: someone may respond positively if you make a suggestion, but is unlikely to point out the opportunity themselves.

Brief Agents Fully

When selling a house through an agent, take him or her around the property and point out the features that you like and have enjoyed. It is likely that those are the features a potential buyer will like, and the agent may not spot them because they have not lived in the property.

Anti-UV Glass Flooring, furniture and decorations are protected from sunlight.

Soundproofing Panels absorb and reduce noise, making rooms quiet and relaxing.

Concealed Lights Nonintrusive fixtures create atmospheric lighting.

Planning Permission Plans to extend through this wall have been approved.

Screened Patio The patio is not overlooked by others, so gives a sense of privacy.

Underfloor Heating Provides comfortable and natural warmth with little intrusion.

Insulation Makes the property more heat-efficient and lowers fuel bills.

Concealed Cupboards Provide storage space without being unsightly.

TIP Ask an agent to show people what you are selling if you are uncomfortable doing it yourself, but define their responsibilities in detail.

Develop Your Negotiating Skills

A good negotiator develops a series of skills that are critical for success. Preparation is also important, as is an expectation that the other side will make concessions.

Prepare Thoroughly

Make sure you have enough time to prepare thoroughly. In some cases, negotiators will attempt to rush you into the face-to-face communication part of the process. This may well be a ploy and you should deal with it in a positive and assertive way. If they use statements like, "We really want this issue settled before summer vacation begins," respond in a way that protects your position. "Yes, it would be good to achieve that, as long as we are able to analyze our situation carefully and complete our preparation work." At some point in the negotiation, the two parties will debate the issues, and you need to understand the logical case for your position. You also need to know a lot about the other party's situation and people before you are in a position to argue your case.

When entering a negotiation, it is rarely possible to be overprepared

Negotiating Skills

SKILL	HOW TO UNDERSTAND IT
Defining objectives	Preparation includes writing down measurable objectives for the negotiation. Objectives must be SMART: specific, measurable, achievable, realistic, and timely.
Setting priorities	Some objectives will be more important than others, both on your side and on the other party's.
Looking at the broad picture	Negotiation is more likely to succeed where both parties are addressing a wide number of major and minor issues.
Communication skills	Negotiation involves talking and listening to the other party to find a mutually acceptable conclusion.

TECHNIQUES *to* practice

Negotiating requires a wide range of skills—and there is no substitute for observation. To really understand negotiation skills and to see them being used together, it is very useful to observe experienced negotiators. In order to get the best understanding of the skills, you need to sit in on a negotiation where you are familiar with the strategy of one of the parties.

1. Take part in the preparation stage of the negotiation so you understand all the issues and process the negotiators use to prepare for it.
2. Ask to sit in as an observer on some of the negotiations and take notes of how the meetings progress.
3. Ask for time to debrief so you can find out how everyone thought the meeting went.

Expect Concessions

If parties have agreed to negotiate, it means they are both looking for a successful conclusion. It is quite likely that the other side will start from the position that they cannot move on certain issues. In response, you will have to take a determined attitude that shows not only that you expect concessions but that you expect them to be significant. Such a positive approach will help to put you in a position of strength. You should remain at all times—in both the preparation and negotiation stages—confident that you can get a much better deal than the original starting point of the other party. Having low expectations about what the other side will concede shows weakness and plays into their hands. Although you are looking for a win/win outcome that suits both sides, ideally your job is to get more concessions out of them than they get from you.

TIP Focus on making logical points rather than using emotional arguments to strengthen your case and win concessions.

2 Plan Your Negotiation

In any contest, victory is likely to go to the better-trained contestant: the side that is fitter in mind or body and better prepared for the contest. Before starting any negotiation, you should aim to go through a set process of preparation that will maximize your chances of success. This chapter will show you how to:

- Identify the results that both sides are striving for and understand your opponent's most probable objectives
- Gather information about your opponent's values, strengths, and weaknesses
- Develop strategies to achieve your objectives and to prepare your team to carry them out.

Agree to Negotiate

Parties agree to negotiate in different ways depending on the level of formality. Once you have agreed to negotiate, you have implied that you can be flexible in order to improve the deal for the other party.

Be Flexible

It is vital in any negotiation for both parties to be flexible. After all, if neither will give in on any issue, the negotiation is bound to fail. Negotiation continues until the whole deal is done and all issues are resolved. For example, if while buying kitchen equipment, you discover that the vendor will not deliver the goods to your home, then you are left facing the unexpected extra cost of arranging delivery. In order to keep you interested, the vendor may have to make a concession by revisiting either the price or their delivery policy. It works the other way, too. No matter how thorough your preparation has been, there may be a better possibility available if you are prepared to listen to an alternative solution. You will need to establish the right balance between flexibility and firmness in order to get the best result for both yourself and the other side.

The Balance Between Flexibility and Firmness

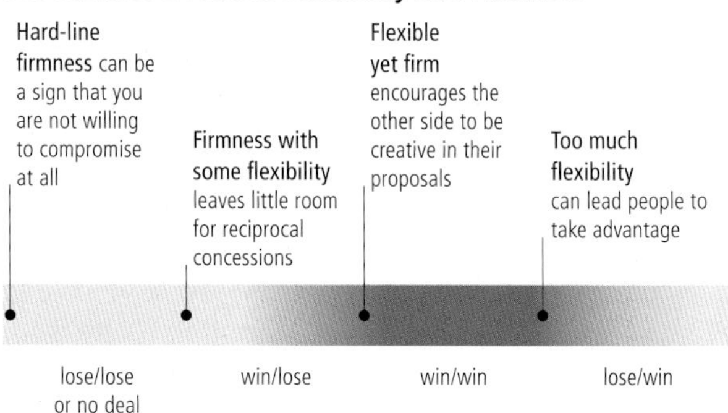

Start with the Right Attitude On a sliding scale between firmness and flexibility, the best position to take is to be flexible, yet firm. This maximizes the opportunities for a mutually satisfactory conclusion and a win/win outcome.

Learn from Previous Negotiations

In your personal and business life, you often negotiate with the same people on a number of occasions, so make sure you learn the lessons from earlier encounters. Remember, however, that the other side will also be learning from your previous patterns of negotiation. It is therefore vital to keep your tactics flexible.

- → Get out the old notes and minutes of previous meetings and look for a pattern of where they made concessions.
- → Talk to other people who were involved in the negotiation.
- → Work out the other party's *modus operandi* and think of different ways to respond at the next negotiation in order to unsettle them.

Allow for Concessions

In your preparation, you will work out exactly what concessions you are, and are not, prepared to make. At this stage, ensure that your mental attitude to making concessions is completely positive. If you believe that anything less than the best possible outcome is unsatisfactory, you will either allow the negotiation to fail or end up feeling that you have lost out. Take a more pragmatic approach by working out what is the least you would settle for, and then regard anything you achieve beyond that as being a bonus. You will not show willingness to make these concessions in the actual face-to-face negotiation, but your preparation will allow for them, when and where they become necessary to move toward a satisfactory conclusion. Agreement at the appropriate time is key to successful negotiating. As Dean Acheson famously said, "Negotiation in the classic diplomatic sense assumes parties are more anxious to agree than disagree."

Negotiate Positively

Successful negotiators are expert communicators. They use good conversational technique to determine what the other person needs and how to meet that need without giving away more than is necessary.

Question Effectively

Asking your opponent questions can reveal much about their negotiating position, although you may have to read between the lines for the really valuable insights. Use open questions, starting with words like "why," "how," "who," and "what" to encourage the other side to talk freely. "Are you happy with your current supplier?" elicits a single word answer, whereas, "How could your supply situation be improved?" requires more explanation. You can encourage the most reticent negotiator to enter a discussion if you use open questions.

CASE study: Interpreting Positions

Mick, a union representative in a distribution company, was arguing that the offer from the employers, Sunita and Ray, used too many rented vehicles during busy periods. Ray started to discuss the cost advantages of rented vehicles when Sunita suggested an adjournment. During the break, Sunita explained to Ray that, as she listened to Mick, she did not believe that the rented vehicles were the real problem. "The real issue," she said, "Is overtime. Mick cannot openly argue for more overtime for his members; so he uses this device." Ray suggested changes in the overtime rota and Mick agreed.

- *Because Sunita had a good understanding of Mick's position, as she listened to his comments she was able to put them in context and appreciate what he really meant, rather than what he was saying. Talking to Ray in private helped her communicate her interpretation without having to address the issue in the open.*
- *By making a concession that was relatively unimportant to him, in exchange for Mick's accepting the rest of the offer, Ray was able to address and resolve Mick's main concern and avoid the lose/lose situation of not using rented vehicles at peak times.*

TECHNIQUES *to* practice

Good listening is a more difficult skill than you might think. Bad listening skills are often the hidden cause of many problems.

It can be easy to hear what you think you are hearing rather than concentrating on the message the person is actually conveying. Luckily, there are plenty of opportunities in everyday life for you to practice focusing your concentration and getting into the habit of hearing what is actually said.

1 Listen to a radio or television news bulletin and practice summarizing back to yourself the key points after each report.
2 When having a discussion with a friend or colleague, repeat back to them what you think you have heard: "So what you're saying is..."

Learn to Listen

You not only have to listen very carefully as the negotiator talks, but you also have to show them that you are listening by looking attentive. Draw people out in a helpful and supportive manner by trying hard to understand what they are saying. If you miss something or do not understand what they have said, apologize and ask them to repeat the point they were making. This "active listening" makes sure that you do not make false assumptions about their position, but also ensures that you do not dominate the conversation and give too much of your position away. Pick up clues from what they are saying to trigger the next set of logical questions, but never interrupt when they are talking. Interrupting a person always sends a clear message—"What I want to say is more important than what you are saying." This is the opposite of good negotiating technique.

> **Negotiating means getting the best of your opponent.**
>
> Marvin Gaye

Maximize Networking Opportunities

Conferences and other industry events are an invaluable source for networking—getting to know other people who work in the same field as you.

Informal contacts can be a good source for gathering intelligence. They can give you both broad impressions and specific facts that could prove useful. You may get invaluable "off the record" information, but make sure you do not use it inappropriately.

→ A recent employee of your biggest competitor could provide inside information about that organization.

→ Someone who has worked with a potential supplier could provide first-hand experience of their work.

→ A recognized expert in your field could be a useful mentor, and introduce you to other leading figures.

→ Being on good, first-hand terms with journalists of your trade newspaper can boost your organization's image and so give you more bargaining power.

→ Meeting newcomers to the industry gives you a chance to assess the new competition.

Informal Networking Conference and industry events are invaluable for networking. Informal contacts are a useful source for gathering information.

Gather Information

A key part of preparation is to gather the information necessary to support your position. An irrefutable argument that shows your opinion on an issue to be correct will help bring the other side toward you.

Be Well-Informed

Gather all the statistics and data you need to support your assertions. Once you have the information, also think about how you are going to present it. It is a good technique to explain complex statistics clearly, so that the other side can understand them. If you are dealing with an organization, get all the information you can about it from the Internet and from its public reports. If you are presenting the business case for an organization to make an investment, it is helpful to compare its profitability and productivity with the rest of the industry. Know as much about the actual people you will be dealing with as you can. For example, suppose you are trying to sell machine tools to a manufacturing company and their negotiators bring in a vice president to one of the sessions. You need to know whether her background is in marketing, production, or finance in order to present your case in a meaningful way.

If, during the negotiation, you realize an assumption you made is wrong, do not hesitate to ask for an adjournment to do some more research. Be careful not to expose too much about your lack of knowledge, or your opponent may resist your request.

5 minute FIX

If you don't get a chance to prepare until you're in their reception area, look at their display literature for:

- A mission statement
- A recent statement from the CEO or president
- Recent press releases
- Any discussion of profitability.

All of these may prove useful—as long as you don't pretend to know more than you do.

Identify Stakeholders

In business-to-business negotiations, there will be one person on each side with responsibility for discussing and agreeing on the deal. However, in most cases there will also be other people who have influence on what that person is able to offer and accept.

These people are stakeholders. For example, where a technology supplier is proposing a new system to an organization, the buyer's team is likely to include a decision-maker, a financial expert responsible for the business case, a technical advisor, and at least one functional manager responsible for implementing the system and ensuring the proposed benefits are achieved. Make sure you have identified all the relevant stakeholders on the other party's side.

Other people on your side may have a say over what you can offer and accept

Negotiate as a Team

Look for the people that you need to work with in order to prepare for a negotiation. If you are selling a technical product, you will need the agreement from your expert that what you intend to propose is possible and will meet your customer's expectations. Your financial controller must also agree that your lowest price limit will give a reasonable return to your organization, and you may need the promise of resources from the relevant manager to support the implementation plan. If your organization has a formal system for getting these agreements, go through it as soon as possible. If not, draw up a list of the people you need to consult. Always get their agreement that the most pessimistic outcome of the negotiation is satisfactory to them, and then try to deliver a better result.

TIP Ensure that the team leader is informed enough to make decisions on terms.

Different Roles in Face-to-Face Negotiations

Within any group negotiation, people will take on different roles in order to engage effectively with the other side, as shown below. Each member of your team must be clear about their role and how it complements those of their colleagues. When allocating roles, you should consider each person's particular strengths, weaknesses, and character. It is common for people to fulfill more than one of these roles. For example, the same person could be both summarizer and hardliner.

Leader Normally the most senior person in the team. Does most of the talking and proposing.

Hardliner Takes a very tough line on everything. Presents the other party with complications.

Good Guy The friendliest person who is closest to the people on the other side.

Summarizer Follows the discussion very carefully and intervenes to keep people on track. Asks clarifying questions and summarizes the situation to date.

Minute-Taker Keeps a comprehensive record of the meeting. Only speaks to remind the meeting of what was said.

Summary: Gathering Information

If you want to come out on top in a negotiation, you must be able to persuade your opponent to concede to your terms. To do this, you need to understand the other party's position—their particular aims, concerns, and pressures—and you need to have all the necessary information to present your case and refute any arguments.

Plan of Action

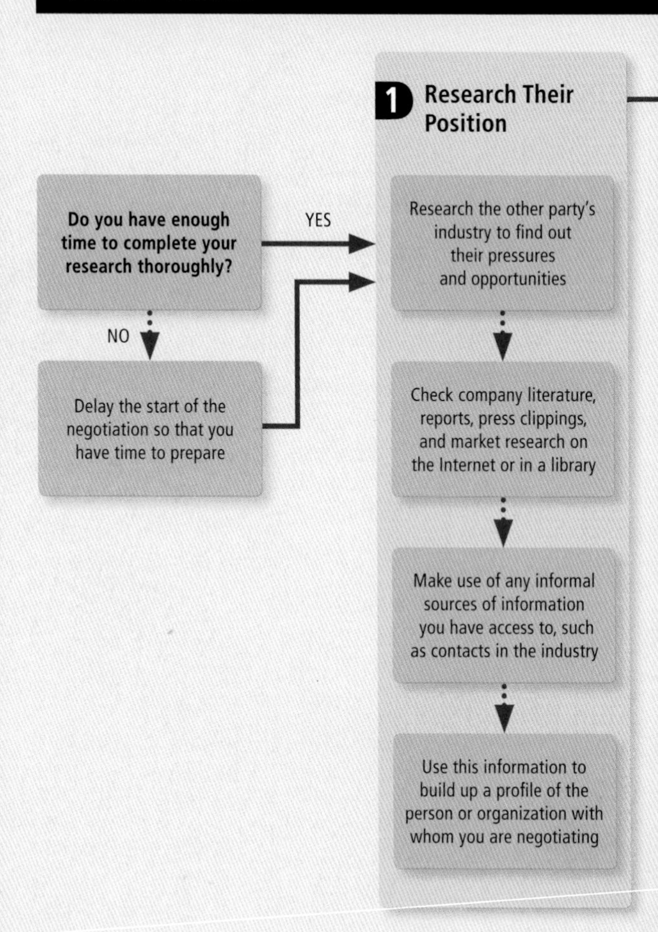

2 Identify All the Stakeholders

Find out the name and position within the organization of each person attending the negotiation

Identify each of their roles and responsibilities, as well as their particular concerns

Identify the decision-maker

Identify the roles, responsibilities, and concerns of any stakeholders who are not attending

3 Research Your Own Case

Gather all the statistics and other data that you need to support your case

Think about any objections the other side may raise, and gather the information you need to refute them

Think about how you can present this information clearly and simply

Ensure that all your team members are fully briefed

Follow the Negotiating Process

Negotiating follows a process. Prepare carefully for each step in the process to ensure a satisfactory outcome. You should have a good idea of your opening proposal before the discussion stage starts.

Discuss the Issues

The discussion step is sometimes known as arguing, but really it is more of an opportunity than an obstacle. Each side gives reasons why they believe something to be true or necessary. It is at this stage that you can find out the other party's knowledge and aspirations from the best source: themselves. It is also an opportunity to check any assumptions you have made about them. They will, of course, be trying to get the same information about you, so prepare convincing lines of logic and other relevant agreements to show how you came to your conclusions. Children, for example, use "other relevant agreements" when they say, "But everyone else has one." This approach provides an answer to a question, but does not give away any useful information about your position.

Follow the Four Stages

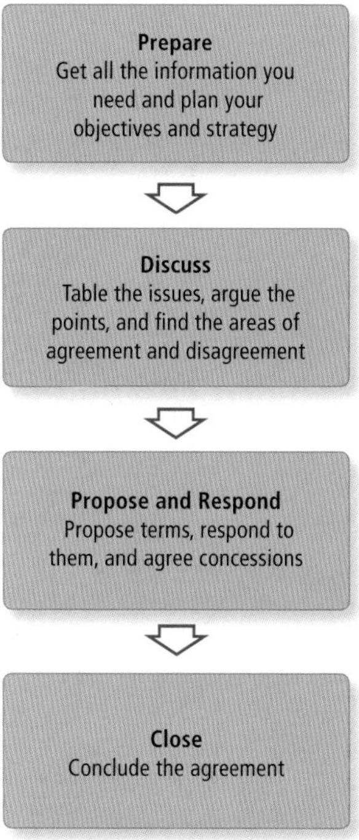

Prepare
Get all the information you need and plan your objectives and strategy

↓

Discuss
Table the issues, argue the points, and find the areas of agreement and disagreement

↓

Propose and Respond
Propose terms, respond to them, and agree concessions

↓

Close
Conclude the agreement

TIP Abandon any totally unrealistic objectives before you start the negotiating process.

Propose and Respond

At some point, either you or the other party will make a proposal, which will be the basis for discussions. The other side's response will show each party how far they have to go to reach an agreement. You should prepare to propose a realistic, but optimistic, package of terms and conditions. If you open one negotiation with an unrealistic offer, people will always expect you to do this and so will not take your proposals seriously. Learn to move slowly, taking several small steps rather than occasional huge jumps. Prepare a consistent set of moves so that your regular opponents will be familiar with your approach and so will know that your opening proposal is not unreasonably far from your actual objective. The more skilled you are at developing a line of logic to support a point, the more convincing your proposals will be. You can easily practice this skill in everyday life, both at work and at home.

Close Successfully

Judging when to close is a fine balancing act

It can be difficult to bring a negotiation to a conclusion. People delay closing because they feel they can get an even better deal by looking for any other available concessions. On the other hand, they may want to come to a conclusion to stop the other side from squeezing any more out of them. Generally speaking, it is in everyone's interests to conclude an agreement as soon as both parties have reached a satisfactory result. However, the ability to judge when this point has been reached is a fine art, and learning to maximize the timing of a close requires practice. The best way to prompt a close is to use positive phrases that emphasize each side's valuable contribution to the proceedings, and then to signal an end to the bargaining stage of the negotiation. Practice in closing will enable you to reach agreements with the other side faster.

Determine Your Boundaries

Before you can set your objectives, you need to define the key boundaries within which you are willing to negotiate. While there is no point in setting an upper boundary so high that is completely unacceptable to the other side, you should nevertheless think in positive terms and be bold. You may not achieve this ideal outcome, but having it clearly in your mind and pushing for it will ensure that you get the most that is practically possible.

The downside limit is the lowest that you will accept. If reaching an agreed outcome means going below this level, then this is the point where you should walk away from the negotiation or find another way to discuss the issues. This boundary should be realistic and be something that you can stick to. If, in the actual negotiation, you are pushed to this point, you do not want to be tempted to concede beyond it. The area between these two boundaries is your area for negotiation.

Define Your Boundaries

When considering where your boundaries lie, ask yourself:

→ "What is the best possible outcome for us from this negotiation?"

Think in positive terms and be bold. For example, if you are negotiating a promotion with your boss, do not limit your boundary to the most junior post at the new level. It is quite possible in most organizations to go up more than one rung at a time.

→ "What is the worst result that I will accept?"

This gives you your downside limit. For example, when negotiating a new job, you may set your limit as not accepting a job if it means that you have to relocate to another city.

The Overlap Between Boundaries

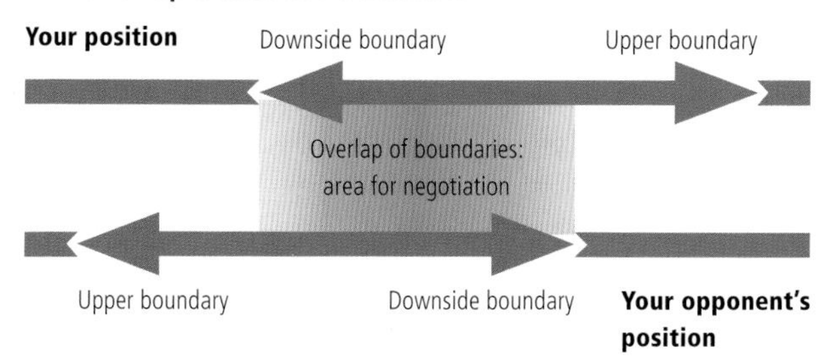

Identify the Other Side's Boundaries

Once you have identified your own boundaries, ask yourself the same questions about your opposition's position. From your history of negotiating with them, or others like them, you will have a good idea of what their case is likely to be. Your research from the preparation stages will also help you understand their main objectives and likely boundaries. You can then compare their limits to your own, in order to identify the areas of overlap and the areas that are most likely to cause contention. It is also useful to remember that the elements of their best possible outcome, which do you least or no harm, are powerful bargaining tools. Be careful not to give them away cheaply.

Comparing Boundaries Each team's upper boundary is their best possible outcome and the downside boundary is their lowest acceptable outcome. They will not negotiate below this point.

Prepare to Negotiate

Set objectives
You must be clear about both your aims and what you believe to be the opposition's

Set your strategy
You need a route map to guide the negotiation toward your objectives

Prepare concessions
If you anticipate concessions, you may be able to limit the damage to your position

Agree on the team plan
The team needs to understand the strategy and each person's role within it

Define Your Objectives

Your negotiation will be more compelling if you have well-defined objectives. With a specific outcome in mind, it is easier to plan responses to the other party's most likely suggestions.

Make Objectives Specific

Negotiating normally involves more than one objective. When you buy a gazebo, you are interested in the quality of the gazebo as well as its price. You may also want to negotiate free delivery and a time scale for erecting it. Define a specific objective with tangible measures for each of your issues. The price of the gazebo is clearly a tangible measure, but you also have to decide how to measure quality. One criterion, for example, may be how protected the lumber is against the weather. List all the issues involved in your negotiation and add specific objectives and measures.

Some objectives are critical; others are merely desirable

Identify Needs and Wants

You must be aware of the distinction between what you want, and what you need. If you are buying a printer for your computer, what you need is a black and white printer to send out printed documents. You may also want the machine to operate as a color scanner so you can scan in your vacation photographs and send them to your family. Separating your needs from your wants will strengthen your position in the negotiation. It is also vital to distinguish your opponent's needs and wants. This will help you to recognize where you may have to make a

---

TIP Think creatively to come up with objectives and ensure that they are clear, but be prepared to drop an objective that has low priority.

Effective Ways to Set Objectives

HIGH IMPACT

- Objectives that you know will be tough but possible for the other party to concede
- Tangible objectives with a precise measure
- Stretching objectives that make the negotiation challenging

NEGATIVE IMPACT

- Objectives set so low that you know you will achieve them before you start
- Vague ideas of what you are hoping to gain
- Unrealistic objectives that will be summarily dismissed

---

concession and where you can stand firm. Watch out in case your opponent conceals their position on needs and wants. They may make it difficult for you to analyze their priorities by trying to persuade you that everything they demand is an urgent need. Prepare questions that will force them to explain the logic behind the "need" to see if it is a necessity or a bluff. Equally, if you decide to bluff, prepare sound reasons for your "needs," too.

TECHNIQUES *to* practice

Successful negotiating requires excellent communication skills, including being able to convey a logical argument. The discussion stage of a negotiation gives you an opportunity to get into the best possible position to make a convincing proposal. Practice developing a line of logic to prove a point:

1. Take an issue where a friend or colleague and you disagree.
2. Prepare a line of logic with supporting information to prove your point.
3. Using this preparation work, discuss the issue with your friend or colleague, and try to come to an agreement.
4. Then discuss the issue with another friend, but this time with you taking the opposite position. This will help you present an argument based on logic, rather than on what you personally believe in.

List All the Minor Issues

In most negotiations, a number of minor issues will be obvious. If your teenage child wants to go to a party that you regard as being more appropriate for older people, it is unlikely you will give a blanket concession that they can go. Rather, you would probably bring in a range of other, more minor issues, for example:

- What time will they have to leave?
- Who will be responsible for transporting them?
- What will they wear?
- Who will go with them to the party?

These are all issues that you can negotiate around so that both of you win—they are allowed to go to the party and you are comfortable that you have taken all the necessary precautions to ensure their safety and well-being. Minor issues are very useful in any negotiation: identify not only the obvious ones, but also others that could be brought into the discussion when appropriate. Phrase an objective for each one.

5 minute FIX

If you do not have much opportunity to prepare before going in to a negotiation, the best ways to maximize your time are:

- List the main negotiable issues that you must address
- Number them in order of importance to you
- Number them in order of importance to your opponent
- Use this to make and demand appropriate concessions.

Set Your Measures

The reason why you are going into a negotiation is because you and the other party have conflicting interests and there is no agreement about how to proceed. Suppose, for example, that you are buying a new kitchen and you want the supplier to install the cabinets using the same people who built them because they have the highest level of skills and understand best how the cabinets work. However, the supplier would prefer you to use a different company to install the kitchen.

think SMART

In a negotiation, confidence can make the difference between success and failure. The key is to be confident in yourself and in your demands.

You are most likely to achieve your ideal outcome if you maintain confidence that your proposal is reasonable and that you are sure you will achieve it. Most people feel a certain obligation to live up to expectations. For example, if the electrician is coming to install some wiring, assume that they will install the light free of charge while they are there. If they decline your suggestion, show considerable surprise and hint that there could be more work for them at a later date.

Furthermore, when they do install kitchens themselves, they use workers with a lower level of skill than those who build them because this reduces the cost of installation and therefore keeps the manufacturing side operating. To settle this conflict, someone is going to have to make a concession. To ensure that you make the concessions that best suit you, assign to each of your objectives a range of three measures:

- **Your ideal outcome** That the company uses their production carpenters to install the kitchen.
- **An acceptable outcome** That a production carpenter supervises the lower-skilled carpenters.
- **Your lowest acceptable outcome** That the lower-skilled carpenters will do the work.

From these statements, you can make the supplier aware that if they refuse to install the kitchen, you will consider the negotiation a failure and walk away. Identifying these three measures also puts you in a more flexible position and provides alternative suggestions for areas in which the supplier may be able to make a concession and therefore avoid a lose/lose outcome.

Know Your Opponent's Objectives

Always assume that the other side is very well prepared and has followed a process similar to yours in setting their objectives and agreeing their acceptable measures.

Gather Intelligence

During the preparation stage, you should get fairly close to understanding the other party's priorities, but you will also learn more about them as discussions proceed. Start a document recording the demands that you expect them to make and adjust it as more information becomes available. Intelligence about the other party's broader position can also strengthen your hand when it reaches the point of exchanging concessions. For example, if you know how easy and cheap it is for the other party to make deliveries, you will realize that they are making no concession at all when they offer to do that.

think SMART

Intelligence can be gathered from first-hand sources, not just published material.

Use conversational skills to talk to those who may be able to offer valuable insight that you could not get anywhere else:

- Ask people in a position similar to your opponent's what their priorities would be—a different customer, for example.
- Speak to those your opponent will represent—in the case of a union representative, speak to people on the shop floor.
- Ask your colleagues for their experience of taking part in similar negotiations.

TIP Role-play the negotiation with a colleague or your boss, with you playing your opponent—it should help you to gain a better insight into their positions.

Analyze the Opposition

Analyzing an organization's broader position can help you anticipate the priorities your opponent will have in setting their objectives.

External Environment

- What are the strengths and weaknesses of their industry?
- Is the market growing, stable, or in decline?
- What are their external opportunities and threats?
- Where does the buying power in the industry lie?

Look at the bigger picture and then focus in on the detail

For example, a large retailer's strategy for negotiating price with suppliers depends on a balance of pressures: price wars with competitors, shareholder value, and suppliers' long-term survival.

Internal Environment

- What are their business objectives?
- What are their strengths and weaknesses in achieving them?
- What attempts are they making to address their weak areas?
- What pressures are the people you are talking to under?
- For what are they rewarded? For what do they receive sanctions?

For example, if a company's main business goal is to offer a first-class service to customers, their key issues are likely to be reliability and the availability of engineers. If staff are rewarded for meeting customer-satisfaction targets, then a production manager may pay your ideal price for a solution to those problems.

Conclusion

Once you have identified the other party's priorities, consider:

- What is their ideal outcome?
- What is an acceptable solution?
- What is the lowest result they could accept?

Differences Within the Team

Any negotiating team will have individual differences of emphasis and this becomes more significant with a larger team. For example, when buying electrical equipment:

Technology Expert: may place heavy priority on how up-to-date the technology is.

Production Manager: may be more concerned with efficiency and reliability than with other features.

Marketing Expert: will want to know how the technology can help the company respond to customer needs.

Finance Manager: may focus on price, rather than be swayed by quality or the range of features offered.

Research and intelligence play an important role here: learning where these differences lie can strengthen your hand when negotiating, as you may be able to trade one person's aspirations for another's. But you must understand the leader's position and be aware of where the authority and power lies within the team.

Look at Their Case

As you look at the issues from the opponent's point of view, you may find an objective they have that does not suit you, but that has a strong case. If you cannot counter the logical case, look for other objections, such as ethical or moral. For example, if a person suggests that they source toys from a particular factory to save costs, you might object, using suggestions that the factory in question has employees working in substandard conditions. In order to save conceding on an issue that is important for achieving your objectives, always try to expose weaknesses in their case. Any objections must be convincing if they are to succeed.

CASE study: Finding Common Ground

Andrew wanted to take a week's vacation at a time when his two colleagues—who would normally cover him—were also scheduled to take time off. He knew that his manager, Lisa, would simply quote the company regulations that one of them always had to be at work. So before approaching her, Andrew looked at the wider situation and prepared a case based on her requirements. He knew that his manager was hoping to fast-track a colleague, Iko, into a position similar to his own. He therefore pointed out to Lisa that if he worked hard before going away, then Iko would be able to cover his role with Lisa's help and coaching, thereby gaining valuable training and experience.

- *By finding common ground between their positions, rather than focusing on the differences, Andrew was able to find a solution that suited both his manager and himself—and also benefited a colleague.*
- *Lisa's flexible attitude meant she listened to Andrew's suggestion with an open mind and was cooperative in reaching an appropriate compromise.*

TIP If possible, learn about negotiating partners by talking to their staff, and if the negotiation was a once-only process, ask the other side for feedback.

Think About Concessions

Most matters, major and minor, are up for discussion in negotiations. Prepare well for those concessions that do the least harm to your position, and think about timing, so the concessions you make have maximum impact.

Plan Your Concessions

Concessions are not a sign of weakness. They need not open the floodgates that allow many others to follow. They are simply a signal that you are looking hard for a compromise to suit both parties. When planning a strategy for concessions, look for an element of surprise: think very broadly about issues that will not cost you much to concede, and that the other side will neither ask for nor expect.

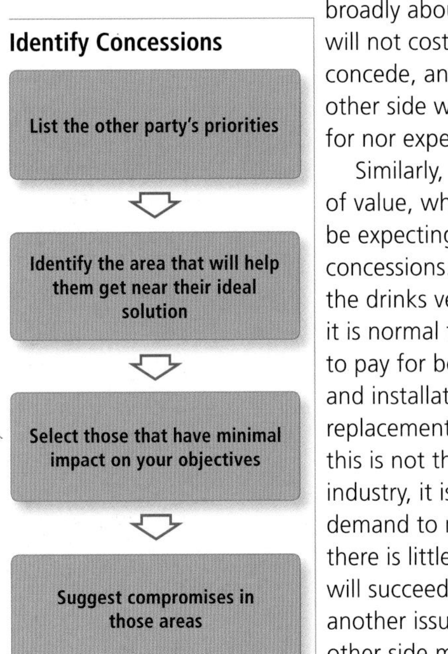

Similarly, consider areas of value, where they will not be expecting demands for concessions. For example, in the drinks vending industry it is normal for the supplier to pay for both the delivery and installation of replacement machines. If this is not the norm in your industry, it is a useful demand to make, even if there is little chance that it will succeed, as it raises another issue. Although the other side may not agree to

> **The most important single fact about a free market is that no exchange takes place unless both parties benefit.**
>
> Milton Friedman

Get Return Concessions

In negotiations, you will be under pressure to concede without discussing ways in which the other party could reciprocate. But you should never give a concession without getting one in return. By learning to be assertive, and to recognize opportunities for return concessions, you can get into the habit of making return demands, even if the other party is not expecting any. This can apply in everyday situations as well as professionally:

- → If your child asks for an ice cream cone, make it dependent on their brushing their teeth that night without objection.
- → If your partner insists on going to see movie A, agree on the grounds that they will see movie B with you next week.

cover these costs, introducing this suggestion into the negotiation allows you to then play that concession off against another that is of more value to you.

Time Your Concessions

If you take a very hard line and are determined to make no concessions until the other side does, you risk ending with no deal and a lose/lose situation. If you make concessions reluctantly and only in return for concessions from the other side, the negotiation is more likely to progress to a win/win result. You may wish to plan the order in which you will make concessions, and prepare appropriate ones to demand in return. In many situations it is possible to present a "closing concession," which could be quite a major issue. Hold it in reserve and use it only at the point when you think it will bring the two parties to agreement.

Concessions can be held back until they are most valuable

Plan Your Negotiating Strategy

Once you know your objectives and have analyzed your opponent's, you are ready to set your strategy and plan the actions for achieving your objectives.

Understand Your Strategy

A negotiating strategy is your route map to success. Ask yourself, "What do we and the other side have to do to get to the point of accepting our terms?" These answers lead to a list of actions, which are the basis of your strategy. Against each action, add a milestone (what the action should achieve), state who is responsible, and a time target. The early part of the strategy can be set in some detail after your first contact with the other side, but other actions may emerge as the strategy unfolds. For example, if you are negotiating a pay raise with your manager, an action may be introducing a piece of external evidence. Make the strategy detailed enough for you to see a clear route to success.

Remember, however, that the other side is not aware of the steps you are planning, and may say or do something that makes a plan unworkable. You may have planned, at step 8, to reduce the price by 10 percent if your opponent buys both items, but their response to previous steps may make step 8 impossible. You therefore need to be flexible and review your strategy as the negotiation proceeds.

Actions and Milestones

Action	Milestone	Responsible	Time
Introduce competitive company's advertisement	Agreement from my manager that my job is better paid elsewhere	Me	During the first meeting

Strategy Document Set out the actions and milestones required to reach your objectives—the details may change later, but it is useful to set them out in writing.

Define an Overview of Your Strategy

A clear overview of your strategy can help you to keep yourself and members of your team on course during the negotiation. An overview should be positive and state why you are going to reach your negotiating objectives.

Write down a sentence that encapsulates why you are going to achieve your negotiating objectives. In order to do this, ask yourself the questions below. If, for example, your team were negotiating the purchase of a new telephone system for your company headquarters, your answers might look like this:

- → **What are the key reasons why the supplier wants this order from our organization at this particular time?**
  They have no customers in our area to act as a reference; they believe that if they get the new system into our office, they will be better placed to get further orders in other locations.
- → **Why should they agree to our objective for the price?**
  Our ideal price is still not the cheapest proposal we have, and the highest acceptable price only just meets our organization's investment rules.
- → **How do the answers to these questions shape into an overview of our strategy?**
  We wish to become a reference site for other potential sales, both externally and internally, by striking a bargain that meets the organization's rules for return on investment.

During negotiations, keep these sentences in the front of your mind to keep a tight focus on your objectives and strategy. Between meetings, check that new actions you are planning are consistent with your strategy.

TIP Make sure you have a comprehensive strategy for even the most straightforward negotiation, but keep it short and flexible.

Communicate Your Strategy

For your strategy to succeed, it is vital that every stakeholder is well informed and understands the strategy in the appropriate amount of detail. If everyone related to the negotiation is clear about the main objectives, it will ensure that no one undermines the negotiation by, for example, making a concession of the wrong type or at the wrong time, or giving the other side information that is inconsistent. It may be that a senior manager, who will be relatively uninvolved in the negotiation, may only need to know the one-sentence summary. Other stakeholders may need to understand every action you have planned and the nature and timing of concessions. Remember, too, that some people may need to understand and have access to the background information you have gathered to support your case. For example, in a trade union negotiation, the leader will have researched the pay structures in other relevant organizations.

Make sure that anyone who is involved with the pay side of the negotiation has access to this material.

Brief Your Team Be sure your team is well briefed and kept informed of any changes. In the heat of the negotiation, one person with out-of-date information could undermine the whole strategy.

TECHNIQUES *to* practice

The role of the minute-taker is crucial when negotiating. They must be able to quote accurately what was said in the past, in order to resolve any conflict about what was discussed and agreed.
The closer the notes are to verbatim minutes, the more convincing the record of events. You can practice this at meetings by volunteering to take notes and writing down as near a word-by-word record as you can:

1. Ask people to repeat what they have said if it was too quick for you to record the first time.
2. Highlight all the agreements made and all the action points agreed, including who will take responsibility for the actions and any time limits.
3. At the end of the meeting, summarize what people said and ask them for agreement that it is an accurate representation of their position.

Keep Your Strategy Consistent

Ask a senior manager from your side to spend a little time at the negotiating table to confirm the importance that they and the organization attach to finding a conclusion acceptable to both sides. They could also take on the role of hardliner to emphasize a particular objective that must be achieved. One way to ensure that no member of the team makes an unintentional proposal is to set a rule that only the team leader may make proposals and respond initially to proposals from the other side. You should also agree to only make proposals that stakeholders know about and delay any others to another meeting so the team can discuss them in detail. This tactic will also avoid your giving your opponent ammunition against you by different team members telling them conflicting information. Such inconsistencies will undermine your argument and lead the other side to question your credibility, not just on that issue, but on your whole negotiating position.

Summary: Preparing Your Strategy

A well-defined strategy is essential to focus your mind on your key objectives and to keep you on course during a negotiation. Use this summary to set out the process you will need to follow in planning what needs to be done to develop the best possible strategy.

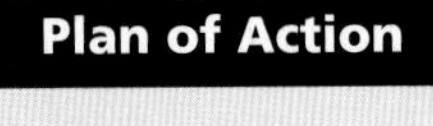

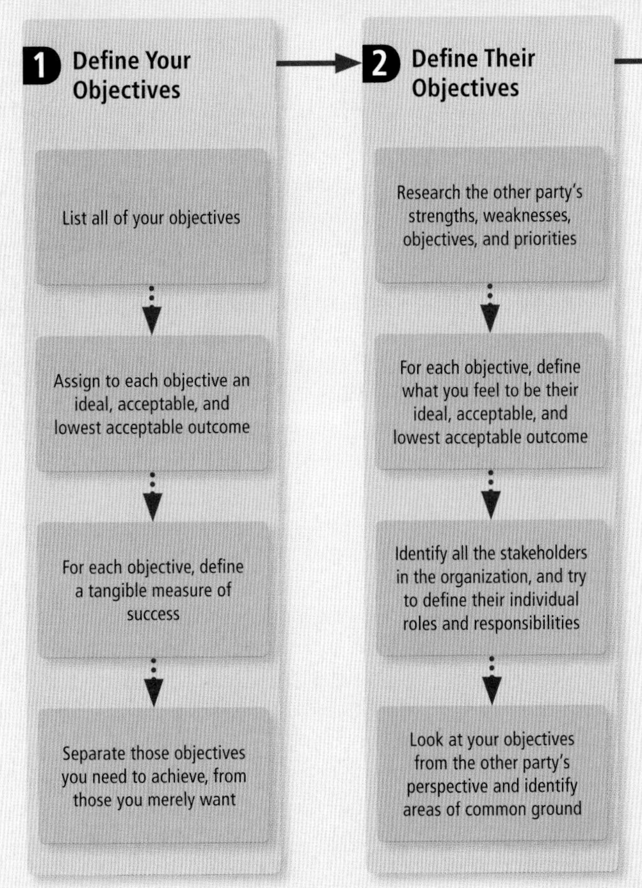

3 Plan Your Concessions

Identify the concessions you can make to help the other party reach its ideal objectives

From these concessions, identify those that also have minimal impact on your own objectives

Plan what you want to get in return for making these concessions

Plan at what stage in the negotiation you intend to introduce each of these concessions

4 Plan Your Strategy

Write down the actions that you need to take in order to reach your objectives

Write down the actions that the other party needs to take if you are to reach your objectives

Next to each action, write a milestone for completion, the person responsible, and the time target

Ensure that each member of your team and all stakeholders are fully briefed

3 Set Up Meetings

You have done your research, defined your objectives, and decided on your strategy; now you are ready to line up your team and prepare for kickoff. As long as you have done your planning thoroughly, you should be able to move smoothly into the phase of face-to-face negotiation. This chapter will show you how you give yourself the advantage by:

- Taking control of the agenda, the negotiating environment, and the time scale
- Thinking about how communication skills and body language can best be used
- Rehearsing your negotiating skills and learning from experiencing
- Optimizing the timing of your proposals.

Organize the Agenda

Strengthen your position by being the side to propose the agenda. You can then order the issues to best reflect your objectives and the strategy you have adopted to achieve them.

Plan the Agenda

To give the negotiation a positive start, plan to begin discussions with any issues agreed upon in the minutes of previous meetings and those that you believe will be relatively straightforward to settle. Then introduce the issues that describe your most important objectives, as everyone will be most alert at this stage of the meeting. Although you should leave the other side's key issues until later, put some minor ones in here that you know to be important to them, to make sure that it is not difficult to persuade them to accept your agenda. If there is a set break, such as a lunch, plan to discuss their key issues right afterward. This will give you the advantage because everyone will be at their lowest energy for the hour or so after lunch.

think SMART

Rather than revealing your entire position at once, it can be a useful tactic to hold back issues: a surprise introduction could lead to an extra concession and allows you to react flexibly to other proposals.

For example, suppose that, as a purchaser, you have achieved a price lying between your ideal and your highest acceptable. You could use a hidden agenda item to reopen discussions:

- "Our engineers are saying that we need 24/7 cover in the remote locations as well as headquarters."
- "We cannot offer 24/7 support in all locations."
- "In that case we need a more attractive price to make it acceptable for us to solve that problem for ourselves."

Word the Agenda Correctly

The aim of negotiation is agreement, so avoid words that appear controversial or biased toward your case. Use positive words that are clearly looking for conciliation, rather than airing grievances:

NEGATIVE PHRASING	POSITIVE PHRASING
"Withdrawal of overtime offer" This sounds aggressive.	**"Reopening of overtime discussion"** This makes the same point in a less challenging fashion.

NEGATIVE PHRASING	POSITIVE PHRASING
"Unauthorized, unofficial action at southern factory" This phrasing will lead to argument and bitterness.	**"Achieving resumption of normal working practice in the south"** This shows that you are looking for a solution, not a battle.

During the actual meeting you may want to be provocative, for example, to put them at a disadvantage if they become upset or angry. Do not introduce such controversy in the agenda, as this will allow them to prepare a strategy for dealing with it.

Consider Including Timings

There are pros and cons to specifying timings that state when parties should have reached agreement on one point and be ready to move on to the next. Including timings means that a sticking point can be "parked" rather than the discussion continuing fruitlessly. It may be that further into the negotiation, that particular point will be resolved in the context of another issue. However, if you want to tactically prolong the negotiation because you anticipate an upcoming improvement in your case, it would be advisable to leave detailed timings out.

Rehearse the Negotiation

Rehearsal is not optional when setting up and running meetings, it is an urgent necessity. Before you can rehearse effectively, you need a comprehensive, accurate understanding of the other side.

Understand Your Opponent

"If you know your enemy and know yourself, you need not fear the result of a hundred battles. If you know yourself but not your enemy, for every victory gained you will also suffer a defeat. If you know neither the enemy nor yourself, you will succumb in every battle."

Thus wrote Sun Tzu in *The Art of War*, but this principle is also relevant in negotiations, where you come in contact with people you may not even have met before and you have to quickly sum them up in order to anticipate how they will react to your proposals. When dealing with a couple, for example, you will get clues about who is more likely to make concessions and who will take a harder line. This enables you to focus on negotiating with the former,

TECHNIQUES *to* practice

A thorough understanding of your opponent will help you to put them at ease, appreciate what they are really saying, and find the best responses to demands. Develop the skill of painting a word portrait of key people on the other side by asking yourself:

- What kind of person are they? Do they seem friendly? Open or self-contained? Are they impulsive or controlled?
- What are their strengths and weaknesses? Do they show attention to detail or are they only interested in the overview? Are they a people manager or project-oriented? Are they a strong negotiator?
- What are their interests outside work? Do they have hobbies? Do they have family?

All this information will put you in the best possible position to deal effectively with that person.

encouraging them to influence their partner into accepting your proposals. Do this in team negotiating as well, and take advantage of any previous contact you or your colleagues have had with the other side to find out as much about them as possible. The more information you have, the more accurate your impressions will be.

Plan and Reflect

As well as gaining experience by being involved in negotiations, you must also carefully plan and reflect on what actually happens, so you learn from your experiences. This is summarized in the process known as PERL, which can be applied in both real and simulated negotiating exercises.

- Plan the negotiation thoroughly.
- Execute the plan, strike a deal, and carry out all the agreed actions.
- Reflect on how the process went and how close you were to achieving your objectives. If possible, discuss it with the other side and identify where you could save time and reach a better outcome.
- Learn from the negotiation. Keep minutes of proceedings for future reference and write your own notes detailing what you learned from both the role-plays and the actual negotiating process.

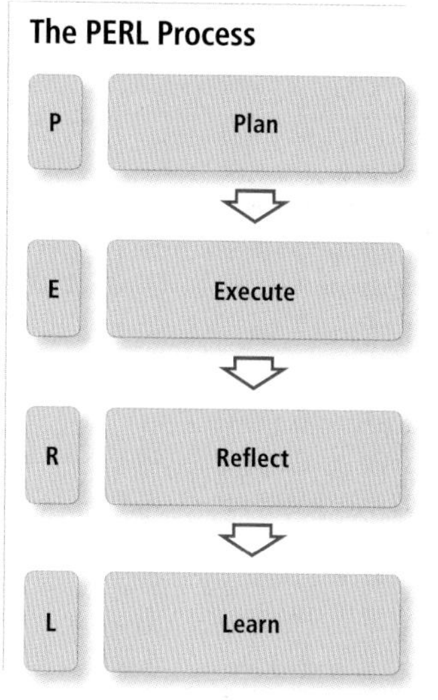

TIP Include time for briefing your team and rehearsing in the negotiating schedule.

Practice Role-Play

Role-play is a powerful tool for preparing for real scenarios. It is extraordinary how much easier it is to field a question if you tried it out the previous day. When you prepare a response in your head, you tend to leave loose ends that you are not entirely sure how to finish off in real life. Role-play forces you to face up to them and find a way to resolve them that is realistic. The exercise may also bring up issues that you may not have otherwise considered. Ask a friend or colleague to help you by enacting the person with whom you will be negotiating, so you can practice putting your own case. Brief them as thoroughly as you can—the more they understand about your opponent, the more easily they will be able to represent them and the more realistic their questions and reactions will be. Remember, only the person playing your opponent is role-playing; you are being yourself and doing your job.

Learn from Small Businesses

People in small businesses and those who work for themselves, such as plumbers and carpenters, need to be skilled negotiators. Learning how such people think and operate can give you valuable insight into how to negotiate:

- → They work on the premise that everything is negotiable: when it comes to the annual agreement of a credit line, for example, make demands from the bank in other areas such as lower charges or lower security requirements.
- → They negotiate frequently: always seek further discounts from suppliers on a regular basis and make it clear that you are prepared to switch suppliers.
- → They exploit salespeople, rather than the other way around: form good relationships with your regular salespeople so you get better deals, but never let them lock you in to poor deals.

Learn from Experiencing

A process of more structured role-play can help you rehearse for a particular negotiation and at the same time improve your negotiating skills and the skills of other people in your organization. Suppose you are about to negotiate the terms and conditions of a catering service with the sales manager of the potential supplier. Once you have gathered information about the person—who is likely to be an experienced negotiator—and you have an understanding of their position, bring together a group of between four and six people from your team for a negotiating workshop. Choose the strongest negotiator to role-play the sales manager and then brief all the delegates so they can each role-play your part in turn. You will learn not only from your own role-play experience, but also from the process of watching several other people attempt the same task, as you will pick up on things you do not notice when doing it yourself.

Structure the Role-Play

In this scenario, the group leader is the person responsible for the real negotiation. The "opposition leader" is a person in your team playing the opponent. The best person to play this role is the most experienced negotiator.

Group leader briefs team on the negotiation; "opposition leader" briefs on their position

Group leader and "opposition leader" role-play negotiation

Feedback from "opposition leader" and rest of group

Each member of group role-plays the negotiation with the "opposition leader"

Feedback from "opposition leader" and rest of group

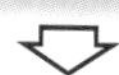

Group leader role-plays negotiation for a second time

Final feedback from group

Communicate Effectively

Before negotiating, make sure your team is well briefed on the strategy. Identify areas likely to cause deadlock and plan how to signal the way to a compromise.

Work as a Team

Negotiating teams can be as small as two or considerably larger. When you have agreed on each member's role in the team, brief them thoroughly and keep them up to date as the negotiation progresses. This avoids contradictory statements that could weaken your case. For example, if you, the leader, have stated clearly that you have full authority to agree on a price, you must avoid your hardliner trying to delay talks by saying he has to confer with head office on price.

Each team member must be clear on the strategy, and their role within it

Use Signals

During the discussion phase of the negotiation, avoid language that leads to deadlock. Use signals to indicate that you may consider moving your position under different circumstances. Consider these two statements:

- "We will never agree to what you are proposing."
- "We will never agree to what you are proposing in its present form."

The first statement is unqualified and leaves no room for maneuver, whereas the second signals that, if the other side amends their offer, it will open up the possibility of agreement. Similarly:

- "We never give discounts" stifles negotiation and risks getting to an impasse.
- "We would find it extremely difficult to meet that delivery date" signals that it is not impossible.

You need to listen hard for the other side's signals. They can come hidden in long sentences, so you need to concentrate on every word.

Watch the Other Side for Clues

Watch for physical clues as to what the other party is thinking; people's body language can give away much more than they intend to reveal.

Anxious to Finish Clock-watching and looking anxious may reveal that they need to close quickly. This could be an opportunity to add a little pressure to get more concessions.

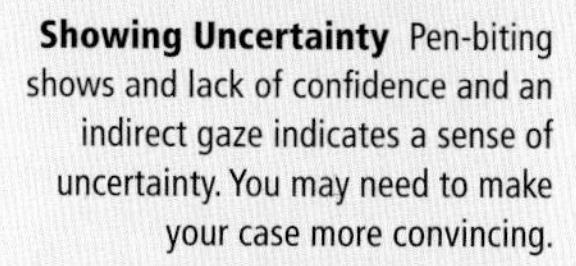

Showing Uncertainty Pen-biting shows and lack of confidence and an indirect gaze indicates a sense of uncertainty. You may need to make your case more convincing.

Uncomfortable They are likely to be at their lowest acceptable limit. If the current offer is not viable for you, consider agreeing to walk away.

TIP Use direct communication and avoid sending an unintended signal, either through what you say or through the way that you say it.

Understand Body Language

We communicate with our bodies as much as with our speech, and it is easy for a person's body language to contradict their verbal message. An understanding of body language can be very helpful when negotiating: you can control your own body language to be sure it is consistent with what you want to say, and it also allows you to gain insight into your opponent's state of mind:

- A positive posture is very open to the other person, and direct eye contact shows confidence and friendliness.
- A more neutral stance can be achieved by standing sideways on, with your arms down by your sides, and by making direct eye contact with the other person.
- Negative body language involves an indirect or evasive gaze. A person pulling their ear or fidgeting is likely to be uncomfortable with the conversation that is taking place. If a person is feeling uncomfortable because they are not telling the truth, they are likely to signal this with an awkward posture.

TECHNIQUES *to* practice

Mirroring is a useful skill to perfect because it puts people at ease.

People feel more comfortable when they think they are dealing with others who are like them. You can see people use mirroring in all kinds of situations—many effective communicators do it naturally. It is an easy skill to learn; a little practice should soon get you proficient enough to try it in meetings.

- Watch people at social gatherings and see how they mirror each other.
- Try mirroring with someone you know well.
- Then try the technique in a business context.

TIP When you are nervous, think of a time in the past when you were really confident and anchor yourself to that memory.

Learn to Mirror

A key skill in nonverbal communication is mirroring. Mirroring body language is based on the fact that we are more at ease, subconsciously, with people who are similar to ourselves. You can mirror most things:

- → **Posture** If they are upright, so are you. If they cross their legs, so do you. Make a mirror image by, for example, crossing your left leg when opposite someone who has crossed their right leg.
- → **Voice** Listen to the tone and speed of their voice and try to respond in the same way. Is their language concise or more detailed? If, for example, they ask a long question, they will be quite comfortable with a detailed answer.
- → **Mood** Pick up on their mood, whether, for example, it is humorous or serious, and then take your lead from them.
- → **Dress** When appropriate, aim to dress as formally or as casually as they do.
- → **Gestures** Mirror the other person's use of gestures when they speak.

Mirror Body Language Reflecting your opponent's posture creates an impression of empathy, which can put you in a stronger negotiating position.

Exploit Your Environment

When setting up a professional environment for face-to-face negotiations, use every advantage you can to help achieve your objectives. Decide on "home or away" and adjust the timing of the negotiation accordingly.

Decide on Home or Away

Generally speaking, it is better to volunteer to be the host at the meetings. This gives you two immediate advantages:

- You can arrange the seating, the agenda, and the timing of breaks
- Because you are on home ground, you have fewer problems if you want to prolong the meeting, whereas the other side has the inconvenience of delaying a long trip home.

There can be an advantage, however, in offering to hold the meeting at the other party's facility. It shows that you are making an effort and hints at your open-mindedness. If the other side is hosting and when you arrive you discover that they have not set an agenda with timings against

think SMART

You can make the most of your home advantage by postponing the negotiation. With multiple teams and control over timing, you can maximize your position to the detriment of the other side.

This ploy has been used in Japan. The negotiating team meets their international visitors at the airport, takes their tickets, and agrees to confirm their return flights so they know exactly when the group is leaving. They then offer the team "time to recover from the flight" and use another team to show the visitors the sights and entertain them lavishly into the night. When the time for negotiating comes, the actual negotiating team is brought in and faces a group of tired and slightly-disoriented executives with a strict timing endpoint.

TIP Make sure you have good facilities for your visual aids, but only supply this equipment for the other side if they have expressly asked for it.

each item, insist that they do. This means that they will have to commit to a finish time, and you therefore avoid being pressured into either reaching a decision quickly or being delayed when you have a long way to travel home.

Look for Advantage

If you are hosting the negotiation, then you can manipulate the atmosphere and environment to suit you, but keep it professional. Have water available and be aware of how to adjust the temperature of the room: lowering it and postponing a break can push people toward looking for a faster conclusion, generally to their disadvantage. Offer alcohol at lunch but never drink it yourself. As host, you have control over arranging the seating plan, which you can also use to your advantage.

Exploit Seating Arrangements

Team Members Together
It is normal to seat two teams facing each other along the edge of a rectangular table, with the two leaders sitting opposite each other in the middle. However, you may decide to put your leader at the head of the table, an implied acknowledgement that the home side is in charge.

Team Members Separated
Alternatively, you could try surprising the other side by mingling some of their team in with yours; such an unusual arrangement can be disconcerting, especially if people lose eye contact with each other. However, make sure that everyone in your team maintains the ability to see each other.

Agree on the Issues

It is likely that teams will have agreed on the issues in advance of the negotiation. Nevertheless, start the meeting by agreeing on the agenda, then sit back, listen, and look for the right time to make a proposal.

Listen to Their Case

As the other side makes their case, listen carefully to their arguments and look for flaws of logic or fact. You could interrupt them to correct an error, leaving them unsure of how to proceed, but this is not usually advisable. In general, it is best to hear their whole case through, without interruptions, so you can fully understand it and identify any discrepancies between your assumptions and their actual position. Make notes of their key points and any issues that you might be able to take advantage of later. Clarify any queries you have by asking questions. You should have as clear an understanding as possible of their position before you start to present your own.

Time Your Proposal

If the negotiation is to come to a satisfactory conclusion, both parties will have to move from discussing and presenting their cases, to the stage of making proposals. Deciding on the best time to make a particular proposal is

Effective Negotiating Techniques

HIGH IMPACT

- Listening carefully to their whole case to check whether their desires are closer to yours than expected
- Changing your strategy if you see a chance of an early compromise
- Highlighting any illogical or factually incorrect arguments that weaken their case

NEGATIVE IMPACT

- Jumping in to argue a point before you have the full story, thereby emphasizing your differences
- Prolonging the talks by ignoring opportunities for compromise
- Postponing the winning of a concession, and thereby risking the opportunity being lost

think SMART

Subtly rewording the other team's position as you summarize it back, without changing the facts, could create an opportunity out of an initial dead-end.

Suppose your customer wants your people to take responsibility for the electrical wiring for a project, while you want them to bring in another organization:

- Their statement: "So, let's be clear that you are going to do the wiring"
- Your summary: "And I understand that you do not want to do the wiring yourself"

This gives you a stronger position later on, to ask them to contract someone else for the wiring work.

a fine art and takes practice, but the best way to approach the issue is to put yourself into your opponent's position by asking yourself:

- Do they have enough information to be able to accept this proposal? If they do not have the right information, they will say so and your proposal will lose momentum. When you make a proposal, you want them to be able to react to it there and then.
- Could they take advantage of your proposal and weaken your case on this or other issues? If this is so, then it is too early to make a proposal. For example, you may make a proposal regarding delivery charges that they accept. However, if you are not yet aware of their position on warehousing, then this could strengthen their hand when you come to discuss warehousing later on.

TIP Make sure the other side realizes that you have made a proposal, by pointing it out to them clearly and unambiguously.

4 Manage Your Negotiation

So, your plan is ready, your team is briefed, the battleground identified and prepared; the time has come to meet the other side. Moving a negotiation forward involves direct contact with the opposition. Keep your policy firm but flexible, as your strategy will almost certainly have to evolve during the negotiating process: "No plan ever survived contact with the enemy intact" is a widely accepted truth. This chapter will help you to:

- Use professional negotiating skills
- Keep control of the negotiating process
- Bring the negotiating process to a satisfactory conclusion.

Make Proposals

How you present a proposal can mean the difference between making progress toward your objectives and pushing the negotiation toward deadlock. Keep early proposals flexible and talk in the other party's terms.

Structure Your Proposal

In the early stages of a negotiation, proposals should be tentative. If you try to shorten the negotiation by going in with your highest wage offer, then you are likely to be disappointed. The other side will not believe that this is as high as you can go and will assume you must have more in reserve beyond your starting point. Tentative proposals can lead to a firm proposal that they might accept, whereas outright firm proposals inevitably lead to rejection. Take the example of buying a used car. If the salesman rushed his pitch and made a price offer below the one on the sticker, you would be suspicious of his motives—why is he in such a rush to sell this car?

TECHNIQUES *to* practice

Being able to propose a remedy, rather than dwelling on a grievance, is an important skill to learn. For example, if you want a maintenance company to put an engineer on-site, you are more likely to succeed if you propose that remedy, rather than just run through a catalog of the things that have gone wrong. You can practice this in any complaint situation—for example, with an airline or a restaurant.

1 Stand back from the situation and assess it from an unemotional point of view.

2 Identify a realistic solution that you feel would effectively remedy the situation.

3 Start the discussion by telling them what you want, rather than airing grievances.

This approach focuses on positive action. You may not get your whole demand, but in most cases you will get more than just an apology.

Make Conditional Proposals

It is important to get in the habit of phrasing proposals in a way that makes them conditional on the other party's doing something, so that you get more room to maneuver. This technique will help to prevent you from giving anything away free in a negotiation, but rather always get something in exchange:

- "If you are prepared to do such and such, we may consider doing this and that."
- Present the condition first, using a strong word such as "do."
- Make your part in the exchange more tentative by using words such as "consider doing."

Use Their Language

Words can have different meanings depending on the industry that is using them. This is particularly true of financial terms: someone may use the term "gross profit, get the reply using "gross margin" and believe they have the same meaning, which they may or may not. Eliminate confusion by defining in writing terms that come up in meetings. If you repeatedly negotiate with the same person or group, use an agreed glossary and keep it up to date. Speak as far as you can in the other side's jargon. This will help to eliminate confusion and show your willingness to see matters from their point of view.

Using their language shows you are eager to see issues from their perspective

TIP Make the opposition feel more comfortable, by coming across as a friendly organization that genuinely wants to reach a compromise.

The First Bid

There is no hard and fast rule as to whether it is best to make or receive the first proposal. If you allow the other side to make the first offer, you may be pleasantly surprised by how close they are to what you were seeking. This then allows you to revise your strategy and set more demanding objectives. Remember that if you open the bidding on any issue, they will assume that the opening proposal is not your best offer. Therefore, you must demand more than you expect to receive, and offer much less than you hope to give. If you often negotiate with the same team, they will interpret your style. For example, do you start high and move significantly, or start more realistically and move only a little? Be consistent: varying your approach can lead to unnecessary misunderstandings, frustration, delays, and acrimony.

If you unexpectedly have to make the opening bid, ask for a five-minute break to consider and clarify your position:

- Identify your main objectives and your strategies for achieving them.
- Consider each side's boundaries and where they overlap.
- Select a proposal that demands more and offers less than you expect to settle for.

Aim High

Research has revealed the advantages of aiming high with an opening bid. Suppose you are negotiating with a potential customer, and your acceptable outcome is selling your product for $1,300. If you open at $1,400 and they respond with $1,000, you are likely to miss your objective and end up settling around $1,200. But if you open instead at $1,800, forcing them to offer, say, $1,200, then your $1,300 becomes highly achievable. Remember to move in small increments. There is no need, for example, to offer a discount of 10 percent as your first response. Start instead with 1 or 2 percent, and even then, offer it grudgingly.

Respect their Position

Just as it is important to give yourself plenty of room for maneuver, always respect the fact that your opponent will want to do the same. Do not, therefore, expect to pin them down immediately after you have made your proposal—if you force them into a corner too early, you will not leave them any options to concede later in the process, which can lead to breakdown and a failure to agree. Avoid using words like "never," making over-assertive statements, or making your opening proposal so extreme that you will look weak if you then give anything away. Instead, ask open questions to find out their initial response: this should not put them under pressure, but it may reveal interesting information if they feel comfortable to comment freely. Keep a balance between giving them time to digest your words and encouraging them to respond. You will secure a better response if you come across as a friendly organization that wants to reach a compromise.

Clarify Your Proposals

Achieve clarity when preparing your proposals by separating the rationale behind each proposal from the proposal itself:

If you can meet the following conditions...

1 Voluntary overtime on Saturdays

2 The use of temporary staff when there are insufficient volunteers

We will be prepared to consider...

1 Offering double time on Saturdays

2 Including Saturday payments for pension calculations in full

Our reasoning behind this is...

1 This way we will offer customers the consistent service they demand

2 Volunteers will have an extra incentive to work on Saturdays

3 The company will save money on temporary staff

Receive Proposals

The other side of making proposals is receiving them. Listen to your opponent's whole case, make sure you have thoroughly understood it, and take it seriously.

Hear the Whole Proposal

There are logical and emotional reasons for not interrupting a person making a proposal. Logically, you may miss an item that makes the whole proposition more attractive. People often leave a concession to the end of their statement so they can start the subsequent discussion on a positive note. Interrupt and you are judging the early part of their proposal without any knowledge of what would have followed. In some cases, interrupting could actually cost you a late concession. Emotionally, no one likes to have their flow interrupted. It feels rude and is, in effect, saying, "What I have to say is more important than what you have to say." This can lead to antagonism and even knee-jerk resistance.

Receiving Proposals

Avoid giving a blanket "no" to the proposal, and likewise, insist on a detailed response from the other side if they respond to you with "not acceptable." A detailed response gives opportunities for signaling possible ways forward. Let the other side know:

- → What parts of their proposal are acceptable
- → What parts of their proposal are not acceptable
- → What areas they therefore have to work on.

Without this feedback, the other side is left knowing that their proposal is unacceptable, but not knowing what they should do next. A blanket "no" with no explanation is useless; it simply brings the negotiation back to arguing or even to break down.

Active Listening Direct eye contact encourages the speaker and a forward, open posture shows engagement and interest. Note down questions to ask, as well as their key points.

Clarify the Proposal

Take their proposal seriously and show that you are taking it seriously. Make notes and summarize their position back to them. This shows you are taking it seriously and concentrates everyone's minds on the issues. If their proposal is close to an acceptable position, it is probably safe to respond, there and then. If not, ask for time to study it further.

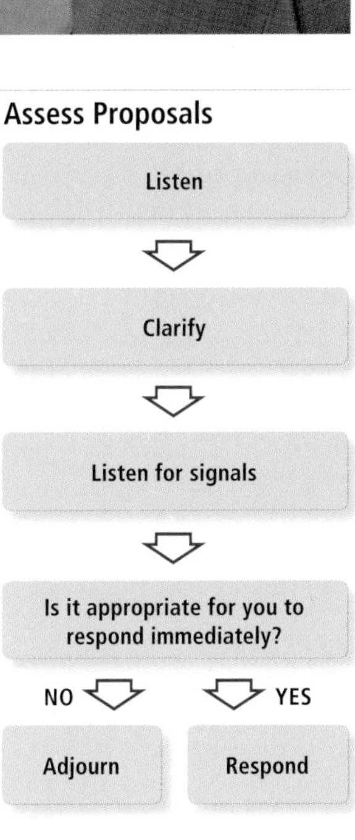

Use Packages of Issues

At some point in the process of proposing, responding, and counter-proposing, each party will have gathered enough information about the other's objectives and concerns to put together a package of issues.

Link Issues in Packages

Packages link issues together to give you more bargaining power. Make sure that you are gaining more by linking issues into a package, rather than offering new concessions. If you link issues, you give yourself more negotiating room later on, whereas if you keep them separate, you narrow your options. For example, if you leave price separate from other issues in the negotiation and you are selling, then all you can do is argue that the benefits to your customer are worth that price or, if you are buying, that they are not. Whereas, if you link price with another issue, such as the delivery date, then you could ask the other side to make a concession on the price in exchange for a different delivery date.

Present Issues in Your Opponent's Terms

Use packages of issues not to offer new concessions, but to re-present the issues in your opponent's terms. Address your package to the objectives and concerns of the other side, and you may find that not only do you not have to make any further concessions, but also that you may be able to withdraw some that you have offered earlier, if the result is likely to be more attractive to the opposition. Think creatively about all the possible variables and then

Effective Language for Packages

HIGH IMPACT

- "We must have ..."
- "Your people will have to...'
- "It is essential that..."

NEGATIVE IMPACT

- "We hope that you will..."
- "We would like..."
- "It would be better if..."

TIP Use packaging to break through difficult issues in the negotiation, but only when you have a clear understanding of their objectives and concerns.

value and present your concessions in the other side's terms. For example, you may be able to resolve a quality issue by linking it to a concern that is important to the other person. You could point out that, if you have to meet that quality specification, you will have to delay delivery by six months. However, if they meet all the additional costs involved, you would be able to reach the required quality on the required delivery date.

Present a Package

Suppose you are negotiating with a trade union that has put in a wage claim far above the rate of inflation—that is their objective. You also know that the people they represent will react badly to any suggestion of job losses; that is their concern. Respond by presenting a package which acknowledges these issues.

Objective + Concern = Package

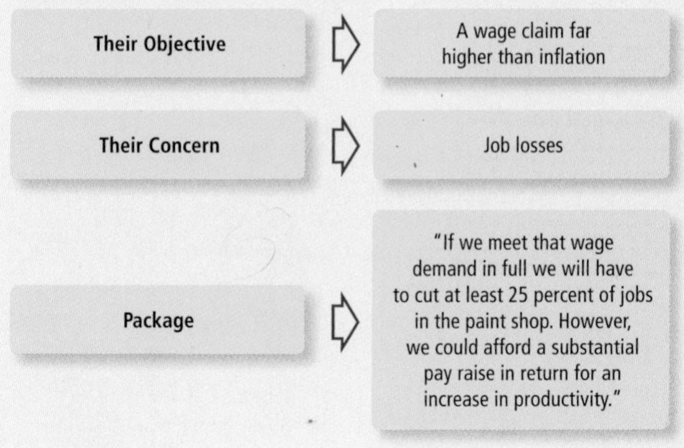

Value Offers and Concessions

If you fail to appreciate the value of your offers and concessions to the other side, you will lose advantage and narrow your negotiating position. For example, suppose you are trying to buy a complex software system from a small consultancy, but you are aware that they will have difficulty in funding the entire project without payments from you part-way through. Although the pattern of payment may not be of concern to you, do not agree to earlier payments too soon in the negotiation to "get it out of the way." Instead, hold it back until that concession can be linked to another, possibly unconnected, issue. For example, later on, in exchange for early payment, you may get the other side to agree to provide for a full-time project manager to be on your site,

Hold back concessions where possible: they may gain value later

CASE study: Identifying Real Concerns

Diana, a mergers and acquisitions director, was trying to buy a small business that the owner, Takeshi, had built up from scratch. Her first offer was refused, as was the next. Diana could not understand why he had rejected what was a very good price. She asked her Chief Executive, Justine, to have lunch with Takeshi. Justine asked him a lot of open questions and discovered that he was very concerned about what he was going to do after he had sold his company. Diana presented a package that bought the company for the original price and invited Takeshi to become the Managing Director of another company in the group, which he happily accepted.

- *Because she took steps to gain insight into Takeshi's position, Diana was able to address his actual concern rather than assuming his concern was price.*
- *By linking two separate issues: price (her objective) and Takeshi's career (his concern), Diana was able to present a package that satisfied both sides.*

or you may be successful when you insist that they take responsibility for implementing the software system in your offices overseas.

Identify a Package

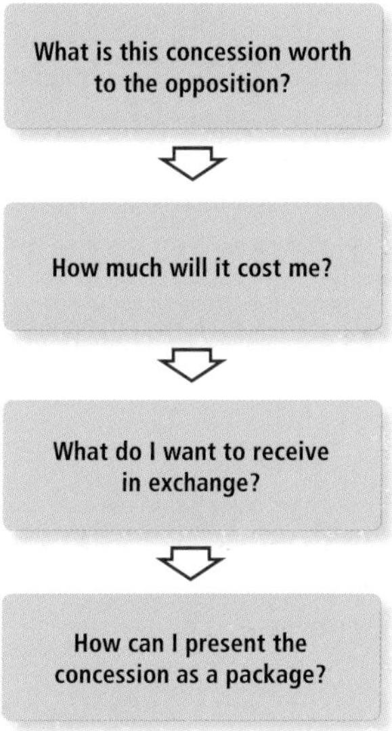

What is this concession worth to the opposition?

↓

How much will it cost me?

↓

What do I want to receive in exchange?

↓

How can I present the concession as a package?

Ask for Adjournments

You may ask for an adjournment of the negotiation at any time. An adjournment gives both sides an opportunity to re-plan their strategy in the light of new developments. If you are presented with a package, a break may be necessary for you to look again at your objectives, and to decide on your next move with your team. This will be particularly necessary if the other side has cleverly linked two previously unconnected issues.

Make sure you do not lose momentum when asking for an adjournment—it can delay negotiations and allow the other side to consult others. In the case of a sales negotiation, remember that any time they are not talking with you, they could be talking to your competition. Always agree on an exact time or date when negotiations will restart after any break. If you leave it vague—for example, "We'll get back to you when we've thoroughly understood your new position"—you risk not being able to reconvene at a time of your choosing.

Adjourning to a different room so the two negotiating leaders can have an informal discussion for, say, ten minutes provides an excellent opportunity to find a way to unblock a stalled negotiation without jeopardizing the negotiating process.

Summary: Dealing with Proposals

No negotiation can proceed without one side making a proposal for the other to react to. Your part in the discussion will depend on whether you make the opening bid, or whether you wait to respond to a proposal from the other side. Each course of action has both advantages and disadvantages. This summary shows you the steps to take to deal with each scenario.

Plan of Action

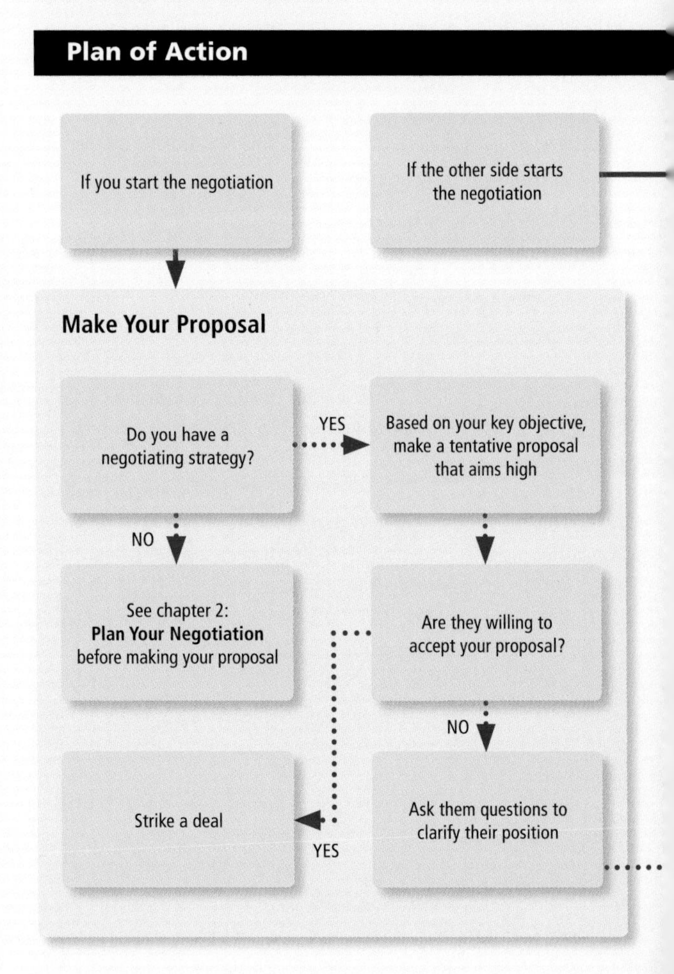

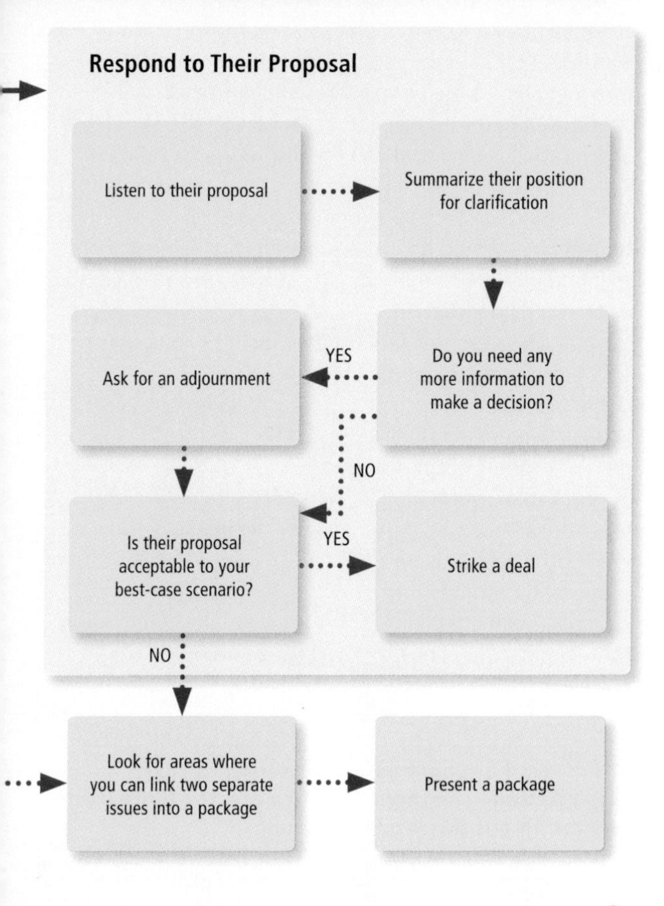
Respond to Their Proposal
Listen to their proposal
Summarize their position for clarification
Ask for an adjournment
YES
Do you need any more information to make a decision?
NO
Is their proposal acceptable to your best-case scenario?
YES
Strike a deal
NO
Look for areas where you can link two separate issues into a package
Present a package

Internal Negotiations

Whether you are negotiating with another organization and people you hardly know, or with your colleagues, the process and the strategy are the same.

Get Support

People in a large organization find themselves negotiating with colleagues for various reasons:

- Applying for resources to join their team
- Trying to improve an offer to a customer
- Applying for a promotion or an increase in their pay and conditions.

Suppose, for example, you want to expand your team by adding two more people. Present your case, concentrating on the benefits that will accrue to your organization if they give you the resources. Calculate what it will cost and then estimate the business return that the organization will receive. If one of the new team members, for example, would be involved in pursuing late payments, estimate how much more quickly invoices will be paid; this gives you a financial benefit. If you are not sure how to work the amount out in detail, ask your financial controller. Finally, get the support of others in your organization at a level similar to yours, who could support your proposal by demonstrating to your boss the benefits that administrators have brought to their teams.

Cost-Benefit Analysis

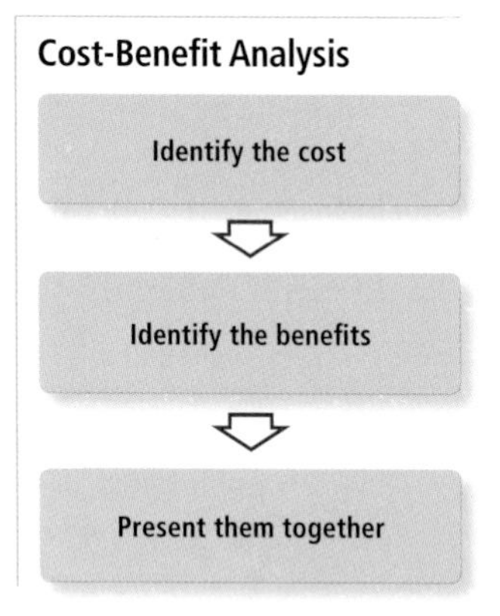

TIP Find a supporter who is senior in your organization—the higher up they are, the more likely you are to get the result you want.

Calculate Risk

In deciding whether to give you further room to negotiate, your organization is weighing up the risks to their performance of the two possibilities—insisting that you maintain your current stance, or allowing you to make concessions. By putting the situation logically, you put your managers in the best possible position to make the right decision for the organization. In a selling situation, make a logical case based on risk and return:

→ **What will happen if we do not make a further concession?** There is a 50 percent chance that we will not get this order.

→ **What will losing this order cost?** The approximate net profit on the deal is $28,000.

→ **And what will be the longer-term consequences?** The order will go to our main competitor and they will be in a stronger position than we are to bid for Phase Two of the project. Our chance factor of getting that order will be less than 50 percent and possibly quite small. The approximate net value of the next phase is $34,000.

Report Your Position

In some cases, you may have to negotiate with your organization so that you can fulfill the demands of external negotiations, such as an offer to a customer, or the quality of products and services. Anticipate these issues as far in advance as possible, and avoid asking for help at particularly busy times. Consider the areas where you want your organization to make a concession in a dispassionate manner, and when you come to present your case to your manager, present the situation logically rather than emotionally. Report your case honestly and openly, and never exaggerate the consequences should your organization decide not to allow you to make the concessions you were hoping for.

Make Your Case

A request for anything—for example, a pay raise—should be made in a logical manner, backed up with good data. Timing is critical: try to ask for an increase at a time when the organization has just benefited from a project you have completed, or an activity that has gone well that you have been involved in. Spend time researching government statistics, recruitment agency websites, and your own personnel department, to work out the range of salaries that your job attracts, so that you can present both internal and external examples supporting your case. Perhaps in your organization, the top quartile of your pay band is restricted to people the company believes will go into high positions faster than their colleagues. You therefore need to show why your experiences, skills, and achievements merit your being within this select group.

Package Your Terms and Conditions

When negotiating your employment terms, think about your employer's objectives and concerns. Their objective is to give you remuneration that suits their profit and loss account, or meets the organization's norms. Their concern is to keep an employee who performs well and is experienced in the role. Present a package:

→ **First address their concern** If you are not able to increase my salary for six months, I will have to speak to the Human Resources department about other roles in the organization.

→ **Now present a package** On the other hand, I am happy to continue with this salary for six months if, during that time, I can go on training courses that increase my skills and value to the organization.

Although your terms and conditions of employment are important issues to negotiate and you should be firm, beware of making threats—after all, no one is indispensable.

Use Leverage

Remember that all discussions involve a range of factors in addition to the primary issue. For example, when negotiating your position, terms, and conditions in your organization, there are a number of issues beyond straight remuneration. Look at your job description and see if an increase in your responsibilities while staying in the same job would improve your value to the organization. For example, if you work in the production department, see how it communicates with Research and Development. Volunteer to take on such a task as an additional contribution to your department's performance. Use that extra contribution to argue for improvements in your terms and conditions, whether a salary increase or alternative benefits. In particular, look for benefits that will offer advantages both to you and your employer:

Any issue has an array of minor issues you can use for leverage

- Working from home, at least part of the week, potentially offers you a much better work/life balance and savings on transportation at little extra cost to your employer.
- Professional training offers advantages to both parties; your employer increases the skills-base of its workforce while you increase your future employability.
- Better health insurance encourages better preventive health care, which could benefit your employer.
- Pensions offer tax advantages for employers as well as employees, so your employer may be more willing to increase contributions than to offer a similar salary increase.
- Extra annual leave may be an attractive option, as long as you can persuade your employer that you are able to arrange sufficient cover while you're away.
- Child care, if you have young children, benefits both parties by making sure that you get to work worry-free.
- Staff discounts are a great way for companies to reward employees at little cost to themselves.

Make Concessions

In the end, a negotiation will only come to a satisfactory conclusion if both sides make concessions. However, never make a concession without demanding one from your opponent in return.

Use Conditional Concessions

There are various ways of offering a concession, and some are more effective than others. The worst possible scenario is to give a concession without getting anything in return. A stronger method is to offer a conditional concession. This is a concession which signals that the other party must concede first and it usually starts with "If...". Consider the three approaches below and notice how each one is stronger than the last.

The strongest approach is to make every concession conditional

- "OK, we will pick up the pallets from the warehouse."
- "Tell you what, we will pick up the pallets from the warehouse, if you will provide someone to help the driver unload them."
- "If you will provide someone to help the driver unload, we will pick up the pallets from the warehouse."

When making a concession, the "If" clause acts as a piece of elastic tied to the condition, enabling you to retract it if your demand is not met.

Look for Concessions

Although you have agreed on a basic list of issues, keep looking for areas where the other party could improve their offer. Think creatively and do not be restricted by the areas that have already been discussed.

Imagine you are a builder who has been called back by a building inspector to replace a joist with a wider one, as spelled out in the actual specification. You will probably have to concede, however logical your argument that the

TIP When negotiating, aim to take control at the beginning and then keep it.

narrower one is doing the job. But if you are then asked to put in an exhaust fan—which was not in the original specification—you can ask the other party to pay for both the fan and the extra labor costs incurred. Whenever possible, allow them to save face as they make a concession. This is particularly important if the other party is being forced to backtrack on a firm position that they took in the past. When you ask for a concession in this type of situation, remind them of the things you have conceded, too—for example, "Since we are no longer insisting on the new support posts, we now expect you to include the paint in the price of the job."

Read Signals Observe how the other team react to each other. Watch out for messages passed through subtle body language—for example, someone indicating to a colleague that they may concede a point. How readily approval is given will help you to know which concession to suggest next.

think SMART

With the right attitude, you can avoid acrimony in the bargaining stages of a negotiation by focusing on the progress achieved rather than on the obstacles.

When concessions are being offered and argued about, it can be useful to remind the other side of the progress you are making. Otherwise the continuing debate can make them feel as though you are never going to reach an agreement. Use positive statements such as, "We've come along way already" or "Although there are still issues outstanding, we have certainly made some good progress."

Modify and Link Conditions

When you first place conditions on an offer, leave room for maneuver so the other party can agree to a modified version, rather than being pressured into accepting a single offer. If, for example, you seek agreement for teams of two electricians—rather than larger teams—to work on live wires, you could link this demand to an offer to increase their overtime rate. This would probably prompt the other party to ask by how much it would be increased, allowing you to then present your lowest acceptable rate. In this way, you have retained flexibility on both issues by making one dependent on the other. If the other party insists on larger teams, you could then reduce the overtime rate offered. However the discussions progress, always keep the two issues linked.

Flexible, linked conditions allow room for maneuver

It is also important to let the other side save face when they make a concession, especially if they had to backtrack on a previously firm position. In order to do this, when asking for a concession in this type of sensitive situation, always remind them of other things that have changed during the negotiation, such as demands that you have retracted. For example, "Since we are no longer insisting on the new support posts, we now expect you to include the paint in the price."

Concede Reluctantly

Never make a concession willingly, even if the concession in question would be easy for you to give away and would not significantly impact on your situation. A rapidly given concession usually makes the other party think that they could have won more. This causes frustration, and may encourage them to either reopen the same issue or look for more concessions. Such a response may also increase their expectations of you in other areas.

TECHNIQUES *to* practice

When negotiating, it is important to learn how to proceed from a tentative proposal to a firm offer. Get a friend or colleague to role-play with you. Ensuring that your body language is positive and open, practice moving smoothly and logically through the three basic negotiating phases:

1. The first phase is the tentative proposal where you suggest that—if the other person will agree to your demand—you will consider doing something in return. This proposal usually begins with "If" and leaves room for maneuver and for the other side to make a counter-offer.
2. The other person responds to your proposal, signaling a possible compromise.
3. This allows you to come back with a firm offer, in which you should first state your condition—which you have modified to increase its attractiveness—along with a definite concession.

The fact that the concession is a firm offer makes it more likely that the negotiation will end in agreement quite quickly.

Link Issues

Avoid the trap of being presented with a list of issues and demands to deal with one by one. This results in the worst possible deal, and you may run out of what you regard as acceptable concessions before all the issues have been presented and discussed. Link issues by suggesting that the other party sets out all their demands at once; this allows you to consider one issue within the context of the others.

Calculate the Value of Concessions

When you prepared your original demands, you probably set out a logical case to prove that they were reasonable. You should do the same when presenting a concession. If you first calculate the cost of your own concession, it is then easier to demand one of equal worth in exchange. Always ensure that the other party understands the reality of what you are conceding, including how it impacts on you, your organization, and your bottom line, both currently and in the long term.

Looking for Links

While negotiating, always try to keep the whole package of issues in your mind, even when they are apparently settled. Concentrating on linking issues helps to ensure that you never give anything away for nothing. Practice this in your home life and you will improve your ability to recognize and exploit links before you agree to any concessions. For example:

- → Children—great at being single-minded when it comes to negotiating—always try to get agreement on single issues—"Can we go swimming tomorrow?"
- → Look for a linkage, however unrelated it may seem—"If you make sure your room is clean by tonight, then a trip to the zoo is a possibility."

CASE study: Keeping Issues Linked

Alan rented the top floor of his gym to Maria, who provided facilities for playing pool. Sensing that Alan was creating a lucrative revenue stream by putting two new gambling machines in a corner of her floor, Maria presented a series of demands: earlier opening on Saturdays, the repainting of the room, and compensation for the loss of space. She presented these one by one and Alan agreed to the first two quickly, but he refused to pay any compensation and the negotiation broke down. Alan agreed to discuss it again but Maria was now in a weaker position: she wanted the two concessions she had received and was prepared to drop her demand for compensation. This time Alan linked all the issues together and clawed back the painting demand.

- *By keeping issues separate, Maria was then cornered over one issue, which left her in a weak bargaining position.*
- *By linking the issues together, Alan timed his concessions well and achieved his objective of only conceding on one issue.*

Achieve Your Essential Objective

Maximize the possibility of achieving your "must-have" objective by linking it to a concession. Suppose that you represent the employers on a project to build houses. One of your must-have objectives is a policy stating that any worker who steals materials from the site will be dismissed. Achieve this objective by making a "final time" concession: the next person caught stealing will face immediate disciplinary procedures. In the ensuing negotiations with the worker's trade representatives, link the issue of the overall principle with the actual case in question. In other words, present the case that, if both sides can reach an agreement, then all such future offenses will mean automatic dismissal, then on this occasion you will give this particular employee another chance.

TIP Avoid bargaining on key issues at the end of the day when your energy levels are low.

Recognize Ploys

Ploys are negative tactics that some people use toward the end of a negotiation. They are aimed at unsettling you and your team on a personal level. Learn to recognize them and deal with them professionally.

Respond to Ploys

Ploys aim to knock people off balance by attacking them personally

At any time in a negotiation, your opposition may use a range of ploys aimed at knocking you and your team off balance, changing the emphasis of the negotiation from your major objectives to theirs, and trying to force you to conclude before you have achieved a satisfactory position. Such tactics will only work if you take what is being said personally, and falsely believe that they are in a stronger position because of these ploys. If you do not respond to ploys promptly, they can drag on and waste valuable time.

Deal with Dishonesty

The ultimate ploy is to lie, and dishonesty damages trust—sometimes to the extent that you want to walk away from the negotiation altogether. If, for example, a salesperson claims to have installed a similar system in another house and, on checking, you find this to be untrue, it may damage their credibility to such an extent that you do not want to do business with them. Alternatively, they may have talked up a previous installation so that you were misled. In that case, you can turn this to your advantage by informing them that you know the truth and using that "error of fact" to cast doubt on all the evidence they have presented to you and thereby gain further concessions.

TIP Watch out for negotiators who are able to mask their ploys so that they sound genuine and reasonable.

Recognize and Respond to Ploys

Ploys are negative tactics, so if you ignore them and continue as though nothing has been said, you may find that they simply disappear.

However, in some circumstances certain actions are advisable, depending on the ploy involved. The most important thing is to not be unsettled or intimidated into making concessions.

- → Your opponent tries to bluff you. In instances like this, politely call their bluff and ask them for evidence.
- → Your opponent tries to divide your team. Avoid this by briefing team members beforehand, and agreeing on a position that is acceptable to all. If differences of opinion do arise, ask for an adjournment and then agree on the position among yourselves.
- → Your opponent intentionally loses his temper. Stay calm and avoid a shouting match. Try to steer the conversation back to the issues through calm, logical argument. If that does not work, suggest an adjournment for people to regain their poise.

Stay in Control Your opponent may try to put you under pressure by stretching negotiations out late into the night. Ask for an adjournment or, if forced to continue, remain calm and in control.

5 Manage the Conclusion

During the bargaining stage of a negotiation, success will depend on the amount of control you are able to exert over the negotiation process. Techniques to help you improve your position and weaken that of the opposition may be crucial. This chapter will help you to:

- Maneuver yourself into a strong position to conclude the deal
- Choose the most appropriate time to finalize the deal, and know what to aim for
- Decide on the best method of conclusion
- Document the agreement in detail and implement what was agreed.

Improve Your Position

Toward the end, get all the concessions you can by a clear and forceful presentation of your arguments, including all the benefits of your proposal to them.

Argue Strongly

Produce your evidence and the reasons for your position logically so the other side agrees that you have a good case. As long as your arguments are as succinct as they can be, do not worry about talking for too long when you present your evidence. When you have made a good point, underline the disadvantages to them of rejecting your proposal. For example, if you are selling high-definition television screens to a hotel chain, produce evidence that a competitive chain is already planning to install the same new technology. Now remind them that they risk losing out to their main competition if they do not speedily accept your proposal.

Point Out the Advantages

Be sure to emphasize the real benefits of accepting your proposal to the other side. Suppose, for example, you are negotiating with a supplier to buy their new range of equipment. Your issues of concern will include not only

Effective Ways to Make Proposals

HIGH IMPACT

- Putting your points forward calmly but assertively
- Taking time to make all the points and adduce the evidence
- Admitting mistakes in your argument quickly and openly
- Using conciliatory words such as "Now, I know that we all want to conclude this successfully"

NEGATIVE IMPACT

- Being arrogant or aggressive
- Getting bored with the discussion or trying to finish too quickly for you to maximize your position
- Covering up mistakes in your argument in the hope that they do not get noticed damages your whole argument when the mistake is discovered

TECHNIQUES *to* practice

In a negotiation, you will make your points more strongly if you can convince the other side of the benefits to them and to their organization.

Practice this in any internal discussions that you have with your manager.

1 Explain to your manager the benefit to them. For example, if you want to go on an expensive training course, it is not enough to argue that it is part of your self-development. You may need to explain how your proposal will help your manager. You might suggest that he or she will be seen as a manager who cares about developing staff skills, and will therefore attract and retain staff more easily.

2 Explain to your manager the benefit to the organization. You might be able to do this in terms of the increased knowledge and subsequent productivity that your training will bring to the company.

price, but also your confidence that the new products will not have any teething problems. Put forward your arguments, based on your previous experience of working with the company:

- When you bought the last range, you experienced problems with the implementation.
- These problems were eventually solved by temporarily putting an engineer from the production department into the installation team.
- In order to avoid this happening again, you want the company to engage an engineer from the outset.

Now show your opponent how this will benefit them: they will gain a satisfied customer who can allay the fears of other prospects about new products having teething problems.

TIP Persuade your opponents that the deal is a good one for you both—you do not "win" a deal, you "make" a deal.

Weaken Their Position

Look for weak points in your opponent's arguments and behavior. Take notes of any error in the facts or logic of their case and plan to use them to seek concessions and achieve your objectives.

Undermine Their Credibility

When you are face to face with the other side, look for opportunities to undermine their credibility and their confidence. You should not make your criticism personal, but rather look for:

- Factual mistakes
- Logical errors
- Inconsistencies in what someone is saying now, compared with what they said earlier
- Inconsistencies between what one person says, compared to another member of their team.

Undermining tactics should target factual errors, not individuals

The inconsistency may be quite subtle. For example, if someone claimed to have the ability to make a decision about a particular issue, but then appears uncomfortable when discussing that point, it may be because they do not in fact have the authority they claimed. In such a case, put them on the spot by asking a direct question:

- "Are you able to say 'Yes' or 'No' to this point without seeking any further authority?"

At best this will make them concede on the point to avoid inconsistency; at worst it will undermine that person's credibility with you and with their team. Whatever the outcome, it will do nothing for their confidence, which could work to your advantage later in the negotiation.

You can get much further with a kind word and a gun than you can with a kind word alone.

Al Capone

Time Your Interjections

Use undermining tactics at the appropriate time, which may not be when your opponent makes a mistake. Such tactics could be more powerful at a later time when your interjection is completely unexpected. If, for example, they have used a statistic selectively, by taking only the part that is supportive of their case, accept it in that form at that point. Then, later on, you can raise questions as to whether those statistics have any downside or hidden problem areas, and cast doubt not only on those particular numbers, but also on all other statistics they have made use of throughout their case. Time counter-proposals carefully. If the other side is used to your asking for time to consider their proposals, you could unsettle them if you come up with a counter-proposal there and then.

Use Stress to Your Advantage

Becoming stressed at tense points in a negotiation can weaken a team's position. Look for signs of stress from opposition people. You will notice changes in their behavior—a punctual person coming back late from breaks, perhaps, or a normally calm person looking edgy and even losing their temper. When you see this:

- Address a number of remarks directly to them to tempt them into making a sudden concession or making a mistake of fact or logical error.
- Avoid an adjournment at this stage since that will give them time to recover their poise.
- Use the opportunity to press for a major concession that moves the negotiation sharply toward your objectives.

Remember to do the opposite if you feel the pressure getting to you or to a member of your team. Take a break, discuss the problem, and resume when you have regained your equilibrium.

Close the Negotiation

Timing a close is a difficult judgment; but one that has to be made if a successful outcome is to be achieved. Aim to make an offer to close when you believe that both parties have achieved an acceptable situation.

Time the Close

As a negotiator, you have two pressures to contend with:

- Continuing the negotiation may allow you to gain more concessions: you can never know exactly what the other party's limits are, so you never know if you could have squeezed any more out of them. But you can never completely eliminate uncertainty.
- Closing the negotiation allows you put an end to the concessions you are making to them.

The first pressure tends to make you prolong a negotiation, the second to curtail it. If neither party attempts to close, then both parties have to continue finding concessions and moving farther away from their most favored position. This can prove to be a very expensive process for both sides.

Signal the End of the Negotiation

Time your close when you feel certain that you have a win/win conclusion. Signal your willingness to close with positive words emphasizing that your opponent's

Effective Ways to Close

HIGH IMPACT

- Stating the close in a way that implies that you will walk away if they do not accept the deal more or less as it stands
- Trying to create the impression that you are at your limit and that is why you want to close
- Keeping to your final offer

NEGATIVE IMPACT

- Making a closing signal that carries no credibility
- Closing and at the same time showing that you have much more room to make concessions
- Making another offer after the one you labeled final, without gaining a significant concession

CASE study: Keeping Objectives in Mind

Nikki, the CEO of a distribution company, was negotiating a pay raise for the drivers. Her two key objectives were to avoid disruption to normal working, and to restructure basic and overtime payments to make it easier to attract and retain staff. The drivers' representatives signaled they were willing to accept settlement earlier than Nikki expected and at a lower cost. She was about to accept when the HR director asked for a short break and pointed out to Nikki that, while the settlement was lower, it did not meet the objective of attracting new staff. Nikki then presented a repackaged solution with a different payment structure and achieved her key objective.

- *Nikki reacted to the unexpected concession without checking that it met her other objectives—which may have been the intention of the other side.*
- *By focusing on her key objectives as she repackaged her proposal, Nikki was still able to take advantage of the drivers' low offer, but in a way that also maximized her benefits.*

contribution has been useful. Emphasize how much your two positions have come toward each other and congratulate both parties for this. Now signal that you are prepared to close off the bargaining stage: "In fact, I think we may be close enough together to look for a final position for coming to an agreement." Watch carefully for their response to this.

- If they appear relieved and happy to close, exploit this by getting a significant concession out of them to close the deal—it could be an extra issue not yet discussed.
- If they tell you it is the wrong time to think about closing, ask them what their outstanding issues are.

Keep your objectives in mind at this time: it is not uncommon for negotiators to see a way of agreeing a difficult issue that does not in fact address their objectives.

TIP Make sure any closing package meets enough of both sides' needs to be acceptable.

The Final Offer

Use a final offer as a lead-in to agreement. This means telling the other side that they must accept your offer as it stands because you have no more to give. To make certain that they accept your final offer as a fact, not a bluff, consider bringing in the most senior stakeholder to make it. Whereas before you might have made proposals from a relaxed seated position, make a final offer standing up, pulling your papers together and even moving around the room preparatory to leaving. Put some emotional urgency into the offer to emphasize that you will not make any further concessions and that it is in their best interests to accept your offer as it is. If you are not serious and they call your bluff by not accepting it, you endanger your credibility not only at this negotiation, but in future ones as well.

The final offer is the lead-in to the closing stage

Questions often lead to silence while the person inwardly debates their response. Even if you are uncomfortable, do not speak, as you will lose the benefit of putting them on the spot to answer your question.

A Summary Close

Use this common type of close to complete the bargaining stage of the negotiation and to move toward agreement. Summarize all the issues, arguments, and agreements that both sides have already come to. Emphasize the issues where you have made the biggest concessions and the benefits they bring to the other side. For example, if you are a builder negotiating a price on a house extension, point out that you agreed to lengthen the stretcher beams as part of the original specification. Highlight the fact that extending the beam as a standalone project would be very expensive, so here the buyer is making a significant saving. At the end, ask them if they agree with your summary.

Make a Summary Close

A summary close is an effective way to close a negotiation. It pulls together all the issues discussed so far and presents a final proposal for closing.

Begin with a conciliatory statement—for example, "This shows how far we've come. Let's make sure we haven't wasted time and effort." Then be prepared to go in one of three directions:

- → If their answer is "Yes" then the deal is done.
- → If their answer is "Yes, but..." and they restate an issue they regard as still open for negotiation, you may opt to try a concession close, "Are you saying that if we move on that outstanding matter you will accept the deal?"
- → If their answer is "Yes, but..." and they make demands in an area you are not prepared to discuss further, you can move to a final offer close, "We have summarized the situation as we see it. We have no further room for maneuver and we would ask you to accept our final offer and sign the contract."

Once you have made your final offer, only agree to reopen negotiations in exchange for a major concession from your opponent.

A Summary Close Standing up to make your summary close helps to emphasize the finality and the urgency of your offer.

A Concession Close

Watch out during the earlier stages of the negotiation for concessions to use as a lever to closing. Keep minor issues open for negotiation right to the end so that you can use one as a concession close—for example, "If you are prepared to accept the deal as it stands, I am prepared to accept your request to photograph the new kitchen for use in your promotional material."

Remember, if you had conceded to such a reasonable and trouble-free request earlier in the negotiation, it would not be available now as a concession close. Avoid giving a concession on a major issue at this stage: it can signal weakness and may be used by the other party not to close the negotiation and come to an agreement, but to reopen the issue and press for further movement in your position.

Another tactic would be to introduce a new concession in an area that has not already been discussed, as a concession close. Its unexpected nature may push the other side into agreement. Deliberately hold back an issue to use as a concession close. For example, when dealing with a small business, use the fact that they are always

TECHNIQUES *to* practice

Using silence after a closing question can be an effective way to assert your will without seeming aggressive. You can practice putting people on the spot and getting the upper hand using silence in everyday situations. For example, asking for a refund in a store. If the cashier is reluctant, wait in silence while they decide on a course of action.

1. Identify situations where you could use this technique, so that you are ready when the opportunity arises.
2. In such a case, be brave enough to stop talking and keep quiet until you have a yes or no answer.
3. Even if the silence makes you uncomfortable, do not start speaking and look the other person directly in the eye.

hungry for cash, "If you accept the rest of these terms, we will pay you 30 percent of the price on delivery." This makes the other party think about how they could use that unexpected cash and makes closing the deal more attractive to them.

5 minute FIX

You won't always have the freedom to stretch a meeting out. If time pressures force you to come to agreement quickly:

- Leave major issues until you have more bargaining power. For now, just try to get them to concede a point of principle that you will be able to exploit in the future.
- To do this, use a closing concession with a condition at the last possible minute. If the other side agrees, they will have conceded on a point of principle. You can then reopen talks at a later stage to exploit and expand on this precedent.

An Alternative Close

In a complex negotiation you may use an alternative close. This involves proposing more than one final packaging of the issues so that the other party can tailor what is on offer to best meet their objectives. The alternative close does not suggest that there is further room for negotiation, just that there is more than one outcome that would be acceptable to you. However, they may come back with a minor change that allows you to move to a concession close without reopening the main negotiation.

It can sometimes be hard for a team to make a decision if the other party is in the room. Offer to leave them alone for five minutes, but always give an exact time when you will return and always keep to it. Otherwise you can let them talk themselves out of the deal, rather than into it.

Never forget the power of silence, that massively disconcerting pause which goes on and on and may at last induce an opponent to babble and backtrack.

Lance Morrow

Consider Late Hits

Experienced negotiators will often squeeze another concession out of a less experienced negotiator by using a late hit. Just before the parties shake hands over the agreement, or even after they have done this, your opponent may introduce another issue or a variation of what was agreed, with the intention of getting you to agree without thinking about it or demanding anything in return. They may use informal words to deceive you into thinking that what they are saying is of little consequence, "Oh, by the way we're assuming that you will thoroughly valet each car after you have completed the service." Treat late hits in exactly the same way that you would treat any new proposal:

A written agreement reduces the chance of disputes later

- Ask clarifying questions to make sure you have understood what is proposed.
- If necessary, ask for time to prepare your response.

Never let the opposition rush you into agreeing a late hit. However, on the other hand, it is a perfectly reasonable tactic for you to use and could result in your gaining another easy concession.

Confirm the Results

The point of negotiation is to reach agreement in areas where conflict exists. Therefore, at the close of a negotiation, there should no longer be any disagreement. At the end of a complicated negotiation—when a sale is agreed on, for example, or the terms and conditions of employment settled for the next year—both sides should

TIP If you can't agree on the terms on a written document, always reopen negotiations rather than leaving any point vague or in dispute.

TECHNIQUES *to* practice

Landing late hits of your own can get you an even better deal. Always plan a late hit at the end of any negotiation.

The key to a successful late hit is to make a significant concession sound completely reasonable, and this does requires a certain degree of chutzpah. Some people are naturally more adept at this than others, but anyone can build up their confidence with a little practice—when ordering goods and services for example, or at work.

1 Once terms have been agreed and you are preparing to leave, introduce your variation or new topic. You might suggest free delivery or for extra products to be "thrown in" for free as part of the transaction.
2 Play it down as something of little consequence, but present it as something that you have every right to expect. Use statements rather than questions: "I'm looking forward to starting the new job; I assume I can continue to work from home on Fridays."

feel good about what they have done along with a certain amount of relief that it is all over. Do not let the euphoria of the moment divert you, however, from finishing the job professionally. The agreement must be documented in detail. For each issue, make sure you have summarized what has been agreed and get the other side to agree on both the spirit and the wording of the summary. All action points must be included, along with who is responsible for each one and any deadlines for completion.

Where you have defined qualitative terms, such as "within a reasonable time," define these in the document or in an appendix to it. If the agreement is not as formal as this, then you can agree these definitions orally, but you should still follow best practice and send a written confirmation after the meeting with a request for your opponent to approve it. A written record helps reduce and resolve claims of "cheating" and "lying" later on.

Implement the Agreement

Once the negotiation is over, the action begins. Work hard to deliver every one of your commitments by managing your team members, resources, and schedules.

Carry Out Your Promises

If you need a team to implement your promises, it is likely that they were not involved in the negotiation, so you must brief them carefully on what is expected of them, by giving them the relevant part of the agreement reached with the other side. Make sure that they have the skills and resources required to play their part. Assign responsibilities and actions to the appropriate people and ensure that they understand the deadlines for delivery. Pay particular attention to any time scale with built-in penalties or those where you received concessions on the grounds of meeting set targets. If significant problems arise on either side, you may have to negotiate further. Manage complex projects by ensuring that there is an effective communication plan in place that keeps you, your team, and the stakeholders on the other side up to date with progress.

think SMART

Rather than fostering a blame culture, encourage your team to "take responsibility" by refusing to approach problems looking for a scapegoat.

Your organizational culture is a factor in your ability to deliver your commitments agreed in the negotiation. When problems arise, focus on what went wrong and what can be learned from the mistake, rather than on apportioning blame. If people are worried about getting in trouble, they will blame others and waste time protecting themselves, whereas if they feel they will get a fair hearing and will be supported when things go wrong, they will be happier to take responsibility for their actions. This no-blame culture is a far more positive approach.

Gantt Chart: Schedule for Building a Website

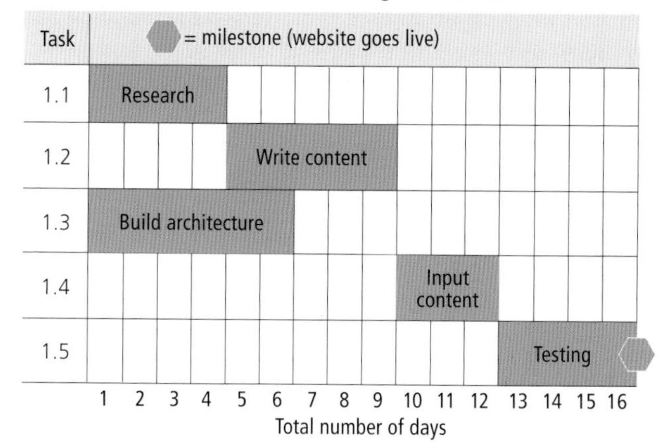

Communicate the Implementation Plan To make sure that everyone involved is aware of their role and how they connect into the whole project, use a visual summary, such as a Gantt chart, to illustrate the activities and the order in which they must be done, and their critical path.

Signal Changes

Let the other side know of any changes in circumstance that may affect your ability to meet your commitments. If you foresee any problems in delivering your agreement, preempt customer dissatisfaction as soon as possible. For example, if you have to deliver imported furniture as part of your contract to refurbish an office, inform your customer the moment you suspect your supplier is not going to meet their deadline. This gives you a chance to readjust that part of the implementation plan and is very much preferable to telling them at the last minute or simply letting them down. Your success at the next negotiation depends on your performance on the last, so work hard to avoid any unwelcome surprises.

TIP Be aware that the other side will remember how you implemented the agreement for much longer than they will remember the actual negotiation.

Summary: Closing the Negotiation

Judging when to close is a fine art: too late and you may give away too much, too soon and you may not achieve your goals. Follow the directions in this summary to make closing as simple and as profitable as possible.

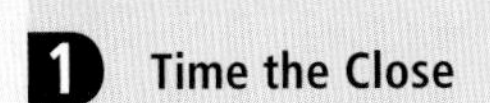

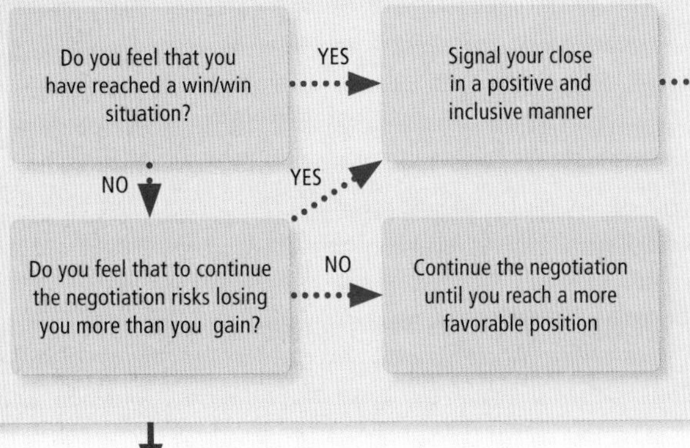

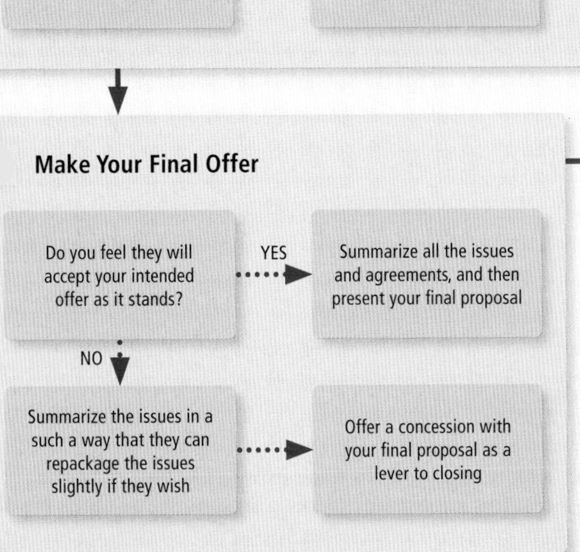

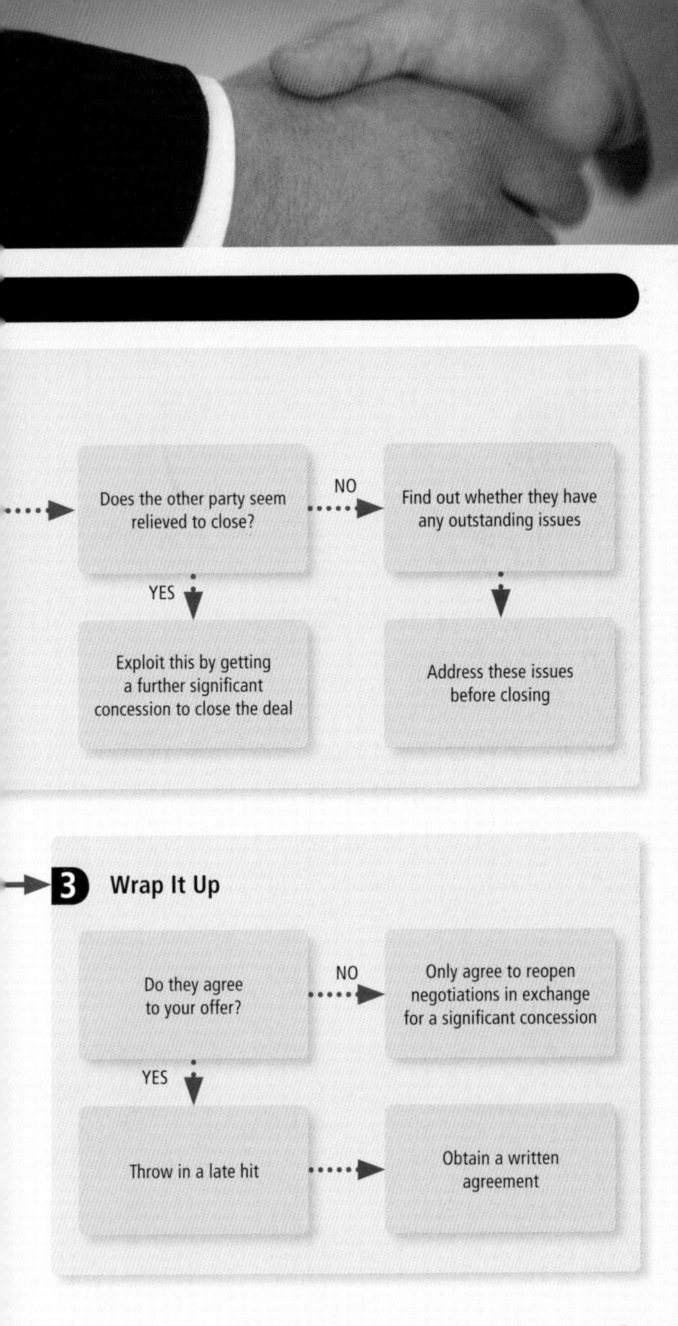
Does the other party seem relieved to close?
NO
Find out whether they have any outstanding issues
YES
Exploit this by getting a further significant concession to close the deal
Address these issues before closing
3 Wrap It Up
Do they agree to your offer?
NO
Only agree to reopen negotiations in exchange for a significant concession
YES
Throw in a late hit
Obtain a written agreement

Index

Picture credits

Key: (c) = center, (r) = right, (l) = left, (t) = top, (b) = below, (tl) = top left, (tc) = top center, (tr) = top right, (bl) below left, (bc) below center, (br) = below right. (cl) = center left, (cr) = center right, (fl) = far left, (fr) = far right.

1 f1 online/Alamy (l), Roger Dixon/DK Images (r), Corbis (c); **2** G. Baden/Zefa/Corbis; **3** Gabe Palmer/Corbis (t), Gen Nishino/Corbis (c), Richard Drury/Getty (b); **5** Tim McGuire/Corbis; **6** eStock Photo/Alamy; **8** Gabe Palmer/Alamy (fl), Corbis (cl), Shiva Twin/Getty (cr), Stock Image/Alamy (fr); **13** Corbis; **15** Gen Nishino/Corbis; **19** Corbis; **23** Andreas von Einsiedel/Redcover.com; **27** Ben Welsh/Zefa/Corbis; **32** Romilly Lockyer/The Image Bank/Getty; **35** Roger Dixon/DK Images; **37** Roger Dixon/DK Images; **48** Roger Dixon/DK Images; **67-69** Roger Dixon/DK Images; **54** Shiva Twin/Getty; **57** Gabe Palmer/Corbis; **59** Herbert Spichtinger/Zefa/Corbis; **75** Gabe Palmer/Corbis; **81** Roger Dixon/DK Images; **87** Gabe Palmer/Alamy; **93** Roger Dixon/DK Images; **99** Betsie van der Meer/Getty; **101** Richard Drury/Getty; **109** Yellow Dog Productions/The Image Bank/Getty; **117** Stock Image/Alamy.

Dorling Kindersley would like to thank the following models: Naqash Baig, Abu Bundu-Kamara, Katie Dock, Caroline D'Souza, Lee Ellwood, Susan Kinsey, Shahid Mahmood, Jenisa Patel, Ann Thompson, Jane Warland, Elizabeth Watson, Steve Western. For further information see www.dkimages.com

Author's Acknowledgments

Writing a book for Dorling Kindersley is a exercise in teamwork. I would like to thank Adèle Hayward and Simon Tuite for their stewardship of the design and the process. Thank you to editors Elizabeth Watson and Tom Broder for their skills, professionalism, and huge contribution. And finally, thank you all for making it such an enjoyable task.

Author's Biography

KEN LANGDON has a background in sales and marketing in the technology industry. As an independent consultant he has trained salespeople and sales managers in the US, Europe, and Australia, and has advised managers on the coaching and appraisal of their staff. He has also provided strategic guidance for companies including computer major Hewlett Packard. Ken is author of a number of books for DK and co-author of several Essential Managers titles, including *Putting Customers First*. He is also one of the authors of DK's *Successful Manager's Handbook*.